How To
Custom Paint Your Motorcycle

How To
Custom Paint Your
Motorcycle

JoAnn Bortles

MOTORBOOKS
INTERNATIONAL

To my husband Jim. He's given calm to the storm that has been my life.

"In reality, kustom painting itself is a warning label."
—Craig Fraser

This book is filled with information about painting processes that have worked for me. Hopefully they will be helpful to all the readers of this book.

First published in 2005 by Motorbooks International, an imprint of MBI Publishing Company, Galtier Plaza, Suite 200, 380 Jackson Street, St. Paul, MN 55101-3885 USA

Motorbooks International titles are also available at discounts in bulk quantity for industrial or sales-promotional use. For details write to Special Sales Manager at Motorbooks International Wholesalers & Distributors, Galtier Plaza, Suite 200, 380 Jackson Street, St. Paul, MN 55101-3885 USA.

ISBN 0-7603-2033-0

Editorial: Darwin Holstrom and Pat Hahn
Design: Mandy Iverson and Rochelle Schultz

Printed in China

On the front cover: The author's Chica-framed gooseneck chopper.

About the author: JoAnn Bortles owns Crazy Horse Painting in Waxhaw, North Carolina, a highly regarded custom paint shop used by many of today's top chopper builders. Bikes she has painted have appeared on the covers of all the major chopper magazines, including *Easyriders* and *American Iron*. An accomplished writer and photographer, JoAnn's articles have appeared in *The Horse* magazine.

CONTENTS

FOREWORD
PHANTASCAPES
THE MANY WORLDS OF JOANN BORTLES

When first meeting JoAnn Bortles you might think that this diminutive ball of bipedal energy cannot possibly be nicknamed Crazy Horse. But she is. In fact, it is only after spending time with JoAnn and watching her work her magic with airbrush and paint that her alter ego emerges and you begin to see the cellular imprint of Native American spirits working through her designs.

This is because JoAnn truly creates her own reality—one paint job at a time. Her swirling airbrush gives birth to phantascapes, fanciful creatures, nightmare visions, and noble inspirations that come from her ability to walk between the worlds with the best Indian spiritwalkers. It is one thing to learn to paint, deal with materials, know the alchemy of paints, and to create the mysterious mixtures that allow JoAnn to give flesh to her two-dimensional fantasies. But the nuts and bolts of working as a successful painter aside, this woman has a lot going on inside her head. She has, as teacher and lecturer Dr. Jean Houston might say, "a rich inner life."

When designing a book on custom motorcycle painting, it helps a great deal to have a woman who has metalflake, candy-apple paint flowing in her veins. Herein, Ms. Bortles will illuminate the arcane wonders of painting motorcycles, from extensive information on flame jobs, through paint design and techniques, to airbrushing detailed murals. JoAnn even goes over the art of airbrushing a pinup girl on your gas tank. She's open-minded like that.

Unlike many "how-to" books on custom painting, JoAnn also goes into detail on what not to do, offering true stories about paint jobs gone bad. She understands that learning the "tricks of the trade" when it comes to custom painting can be very frustrating and discouraging at times. In this tome, JoAnn takes you gently by the hand, explains that sometimes there will be difficult times during this process, and teaches you how to deal with setbacks without going postal.

The woman known as Crazy Horse began painting back in 1979, mixing her lifelong love of art with her other love: cars and motorcycles. Y'see, JoAnn is proud to be a true gearhead and was the only female moto-junkie in her high school welding broken bike parts together in shop class. When she started doing custom paint, she was one of the only women on the East Coast involved with painting and riding custom motorcycles. She recently told me, "Looking through my old painting books, there are no women in them. Not a one."

JoAnn has worn many hats over the years, from inspecting F-100 jet engines to welding the oil pans on IROC racecars. She has traveled extensively, but painting bikes has been the one constant and passion in her life for the past 25 years. She says, "Sitting down, airbrush in hand, gives me comfort. Over the years I have seen many changes in bike painting, trends that come and go and come again."

But JoAnn also has the ability to see ahead of the custom curve, knowing instinctively what is coming around the next bend on the two-wheeled road. Her custom paint work graces the sheet metal of many of the world's very best custom bikes by today's master builders, including her husband, Jim Bortles. She says that working on Jimmy's bikes has also improved her abilities and style, because she enjoys helping to bring his creations to life. I have had the honor of showcasing much of JoAnn's work, as seen in custom bike features in *Easyriders* and *V-Twin* magazines over the years.

Today, there are many women emerging in the custom motorcycle paint arena, but JoAnn was truly one of the first. She's dealt with her share of big, tough bikers—many who gave her a hard time because she is a woman—and came through it all with grace and sage advice for others on the path. So, listen to Crazy Horse as she weaves this dream of making something miraculous from nothing but the ether. She is a true treasure of the custom world.

May this book inspire you to greatness.

Dave Nichols
Editor-in-chief, *Easyriders* and *V-Twin* magazines

ACKNOWLEDGMENTS

The more spectacular photos in this book are by photographer Aaron Stevenson of Charlotte, North Carolina. Every studio shot is his work.

Many thanks to Dan-Am Sata USA. Their spray equipment makes my life easier and they are wonderful people.

And more thanks to

Dave Nichols, Scott McCool, and Jeff Moore of *Easyriders*

Click Baldwin of Carolina Harley Davidson

Chris Maida of *American Iron*

Hank McQueeny, Ralph Janus, Geno Dipol, and the rest of the staff at *The Horse BackStreet Choppers*

Keith Ball

Mike Lichter

Jon Kosmoski

Darwin Holmstrom

Tony Larimer

Wayne Springs

Kevin O' Malley

Angie Campo Pellitier

Sheri Tashjian Vega

Ginny Ross Jefferies

And very special thanks to MaryAnn Surette Beattie

Aaron Stevenson

INTRODUCTION

The painting that got me into Parson's School of Design.

The 1970s was a great time to be a teenager who was interested in custom painting. Wild and weird paint was everywhere, from vans to chopped-out bikes. I would ride around in my dad's auto parts delivery truck, reading car and bike magazines while he delivered parts and yakked for hours on end with his customers.

I was always into custom bikes. I can even remember the first time I saw a chopped bike. I was 3 years old. I heard this loud rumble down by the entrance to the river bridge, just beyond my backyard. I toddled out to the bluff that overlooked the bridge just as fast as my little legs could carry me. As I came up to the bluff, I saw a two-wheeled extreme creation roaring across the bridge. A man with long, wild, dark hair, dressed head to foot in black leather, sat back on that scooter, looking like he was enjoying life at a level like no one I'd ever seen. I immediately knew that's what I wanted.

But a very bad head injury that year robbed me of my sense of balance, and it would be many years before I could even ride a bicycle, let alone a motorcycle. I'd spend Saturday nights at my best friend Donna's house. It was next door to a club called the Polish Home. Sleek, dangerous-looking bikes would come and go all night long. Donna and I would sneak out of bed, creep out to the front porch, and watch the guys do burnouts. Mostly they would just hang out leaning on their rides, having . . . shall we say . . . very "animated" discussions.

I grew up drawing. My mom dragged me off for art lessons at age 2, but at heart I was a gearhead, a gearhead who drew. My contribution to the high school senior class art calendar was a pen-and-ink drawing of a '57 Chevy. After high school, I attended Parson's School of Design in New York City.

Parson's was the premier school in the country for commercial artists. I was in awe of the talented kids in my class. I tended bar at night, had adventures till dawn, and barely made it to class during the day. But I learned a lot that year. It was a school that taught how to function under pressure, how to stay creative and get the job done, even when the sky is crashing down around you. It was a skill that would come in very handy later.

My dad had bought me an airbrush, and I began to use it on whatever school project I could. I would have loved to stay at Parson's, but family money problems required that I move home and get a second shift job in a local diesel pump factory.

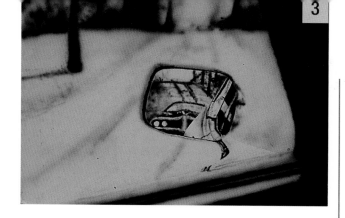

Art school project.

The first bike tank paint I ever completed.

I bought a couple of old Mustangs and began to play around restoring them. That was when I learned to use spray guns and body shop equipment. My first painting experiences did not go smoothly, and I flung the paint gun a few times. I think the marks are still on the wall of my dad's garage where it hit. Then a high school bud at the factory said to me, "If you're such a hot shot artist, why don't you paint my bike?" So I did a mural on his sporty's tank. It was gorgeous. I couldn't believe how well it turned out for my first attempt. It was ready for clear coat, but one night at work he said something truly awful about a friend of mine. As a loyal friend, I demanded he take it back. (It didn't matter that what he said was true—that she was looser than a fender bolt on an old Harley shovelhead.) I told him if he didn't take it back, I'd remove the freshly painted mural. He refused, so I got out the buffer. Goodbye, perfect mural. He was stunned when I drove up to his front door and flung the tank at him. He'd thought I had been bluffing. I hadn't been bluffing—I'd been buffing! And, I'd taught myself a good lesson.

The motorcycle world was a hard one for women, at least in 1979, and I wasn't about to take guff from anybody, not even from a friend since ninth grade. Bikes didn't become acceptable until the mid 1990s, and it was a very different world back before then. Wearing a black leather jacket labeled a person a hoodlum. While working at the airport fueling planes, I was forbidden by my boss to wear my bike jacket, lest someone take me for a criminal. I've even been pulled over at gunpoint by a lawman who spotted the black leather and saw trouble. Painting bikes was not respectable.

I learned a whole lot over the next 16 years. In that time I worked alongside other painters, shared techniques, and developed new ones with guys who painted in dusty garages and basements, and obtained some of the most flawless clear coats you'll ever see. "We don't need no stinkin' downdraft booth." One guy, Dave, the best bike painter I have ever known, painted in a small empty spot in the middle of the nastiest, dirtiest shop I'd ever seen. He had this crazy pipe dream for us to move to Florida and become famous bike painters. 'We'd make the cover of *Easyriders* I bet!' Unfortunately, he never saw his dream come true. Following his untimely death, I moved to Florida where, among awesome bike painters like Dawne Holmes and Chris Cruz, I competed in bike shows and started winning. My style began to really develop and evolve into something uniquely my own. I also met the man who would become my husband, bike builder Jim Bortles.

Airbrushing of my first Mustang.

JoAnn circa 1981 "My '66 Mustang, the first car I ever painted. I ran a 302 motor with closed-chambered 289 heads and a four-speed toploader tranny. This car was brutal. The second car I would paint sits behind it, a '69 Mustang with a 351 Cleveland Cobra Jet motor. My tomboy look would not last."

My sporty tank I painted in 1996

Tank from Stevie Ray Vaughan Panhead.

After 14 months in the south Florida pressure pit, we moved north to a 6-acre ranch in Waxhaw, North Carolina. Jim builds bikes in our little shop next to the house. It's a quiet, healing place, where I do some of the best artwork I've ever done. It's worlds away from those dark days so long ago that supplied the many brutal, savage lessons in the harsh realities of custom painting.

At my first major bike show in 1998, the *Easyriders* Bike Show, bikes I painted took home five trophies: a First Place Best of Show, two first places, a second place, and a third place. **See fig. 8**. At the 1998 Easyriders Bike Show Finals, the Stevie Ray Vaughan panhead I painted took Second Place Best of Show, and this led to five articles in *Easyriders* magazine. Several of the bikes I painted even made the cover. Finally, I was on the map—my buddy Dave's dream had come true.

Since that time, I've had many magazine features and bike

JoAnn's hardtail gooseneck. Aaron Stevenson

show wins, the latest being a very special win for me. All my years I had watched other people's bikes win the major shows. **See fig. 9**. I had recently finished my own ground-up, custom-built bike: a hardtail gooseneck. I entered it in the 2003 *Easyriders* Show in Charlotte, one of the toughest shows to win. There were 159 bikes that competed for 13 trophies.

I didn't think I had a chance in hell against so many high-dollar creations from across the East Coast. But my bike took Second Place Best Street Custom. Paul Yaffe was there when I got the trophy, waiting to congratulate me—I had used his pipes and Z Bars on the bike. The chopper can be seen on the cover of the September 2004 issue of *Easyriders*. It was the kind of moment my old buddy Dave always talked about while he was pipe dreaming in my parent's backyard.

In addition to painting, I freelance for *Easyriders*, am on staff at *The Horse Back Street Choppers* magazine, and am also on staff at *Bikernet*, the most popular biker website in the world. At Sturgis in 2003, I hooked up with an editor from Motorbooks International and started a series of motorcycle painting books. Now all those days I spent in painting hell finally mean something—base theory, lessons learned, and helpful tips I can pass on—so other painters don't have to suffer as I did.

I couldn't even count the number of "how-to-paint" books out there, but I think I've read them all, starting with those car mags I read in my dad's truck so very long ago. I can't help but pick up a magazine cover that mentions any kind of painting how-to tips. And truthfully, I've gleaned some sort of helpful insights from most of them. But there is one thing that most of them lack: Custom paint involves breaking the rules. Deviating from a standard set of rules, mixing paint, colors, and techniques that were never meant to be used together—that is what produces truly original and head-popping paintwork.

Unfortunately, breaking the rules also involves screwing up, making mistakes you won't see until you've invested countless hours and money into the job. Imagine standing there, paint gun in hand, ready to finish your master-piece, only to discover you're looking at a serious flaw that has just set you back a week on that job. The risks you take trying to create unique paint jobs can also create great stress and hardship. Or you're so busy trying to make the deadline, you can't see the disaster approaching until it smacks you in the face. Tight deadlines can kill a good paint job.

Infamous hitch hiker mural.

They can turn what could have been a great job into a passable job. Sometimes a third of the way into the job, you see a better way to do the artwork, a different approach that is way better than what you were doing. But there's no time to redo what you've already done.

Any painter who says he's never screwed up is lying. My butt has been saved quite a few times by other painters who helped me over those rough spots. Then there were times when I had to tough it out alone, figure a way out of the hellish mess I was in. In this book, I will instruct in painting and airbrush techniques, but I will have a special focus on how *not* to screw up: the things to look for to keep from being bitten on the butt. In my years of painting, I've made every mistake that can be made and have invented even more. I've been the one with paint gun in hand on a Friday night, feeling faint, with a customer due to pick up the job Monday morning, and my bank account expecting a deposit to cover the checks that have already gone out. And there I am, standing there, looking at a mistake that will take more than one weekend to fix. It's enough to make you want to just run away screaming into the night. But somehow, I got through it again and again. Funny thing, if someone had told me years ago that I'd write a book about how to do custom painting, I'd have thought they were nuts.

I have limited space to work with for this book. I can't include everything I want to or know. So for now I'm going thoroughly through the books that are already out there and focusing on the processes that are lacking in them. So forgive me if I don't cover every kind of painting or artwork situation. There will be upcoming books that cover other aspects of basic motorcycle painting. Please feel free to send me feedback, as there might even be a book that covers other custom techniques I had to leave out of this book. You're the painter—let me know what you want and need to know. And welcome to the pleasuredome of paint!

Having fun on the road with my riding buddy Angie.

One of perks of this business is the people I get to meet. Me with Billy Lane.

Front and rear view of JoAnn's favorite front fender.

With Jon Kosmoski—founder of House of Kolor.

CHAPTER 1
THE RULES—PAINTING BASICS AND THEORY

Painter's emergency kit.

The above photo is meant to be funny, but there have been times when this stuff looked really good to me, especially the shotgun. One small painting error can lead to what feels like a lifetime in painting hell.

A great paint job starts with a good, solid foundation. The paint on top is only as good as what's beneath it, and most troubles that occur evolve from below the surface. This book will focus on custom painting and airbrushing. Prep, bodywork, and in-depth painting basics will be covered in a future book. For now, I'll quickly go over priming and some of my favorite stress-free painting equipment.

THE RULES
Rule Number 1. *When in doubt, sandblast!* Trying to salvage a ruined paint job wastes too many hours. If the paint wrinkles, lifts, bubbles, or does anything that has you ready for smelling salts or scratching your head wondering where you went wrong, just head for the sandblaster and start over. I have made a few great saves in this department (see Chapter 16, Troubleshooting), but I have squandered far too much time on questionable paint jobs. These hours would have been better spent on a paint job I didn't have to worry about having problems with later. I knew my mistake, knew how to avoid it, and should have started over. Then I never would have had to worry about the phone ringing, hearing a customer say, "What is this little mark in my paint? It seems to be growing."

Rule Number 2. *The best offense is a good defense.* This holds true in painting, from making sure you have a solid foundation under all those beautiful top coats to little things like having plenty of clear coat over your base coats. The biggest advantage of plenty of clear coats is that if the artwork is somehow less than desirable, you can simply remove the artwork by wet sanding it off with 600 grit and then start over, saving the base paint. On the other hand, if liquid stencil mask was used for artwork, then there may be slight lines from cutting the stencil. But plenty of clear coat will allow you to sand most of those lines away and maybe cover the rest with retouching.

Rule Number 3. *Shortcuts suck.* A good foundation and proper paint process will save your life. You'll worry less and have fewer problems to deal with because you did things the right way. A botched shortcut kills, or at least it seems like you're dying. Most custom painters are self-employed. They carry the whole load when something goes wrong, and reap the benefits when everything goes right. Shutting down the shop and going home at a decent hour is one of the best experiences there is, compared to suffering through too many torturous long nights into the morning hours due to mistakes. Don't take shortcuts.

Rule Number 4. *Clean your paint gun, no matter how beat you are, no matter how late it is.* When it's 2 a.m. and you've been at it since 7 in the morning, give that gun a through cleaning before you shut down the shop.

Just a few of my test pieces.

Rule Number 5 (fig. 2). *Test your color and artwork techniques, and save your butt.* This is one of the biggest mistakes even a good, experienced painter can make. In most cases, I make sample pieces with color and artwork choices. Say I need to spray a red flake. I'll do several test panels trying out base coat and candy coat combos—varying the kind of base flake I use and the amounts of candy toner I use in the top coat. Making it up as you go doesn't always have a happy ending. Testing helps ensure there are no surprises after you've sprayed 10 coats of material. Fine-tune your paint to get the most effective result. Always know your choices, and then let your customers choose the one they prefer. Make a recommendation, but let them make the final choice, and have them sign off on the sample. That way, at payment time, if they decide it's not the color they want, you don't eat it.

Do not handle parts from top surfaces.

Rule Number 6. *Wash your hands.* Contaminants transferred from the hands cause many of the pesky paint surface problems. Using a mild liquid soap along with lots of rinsing gets the best results. Keep a pump container of liquid soap right there at the sink. Some painters wear gloves, whether latex, vinyl, or cotton. I, unfortunately, cannot airbrush, wet sand, or tape off parts wearing gloves. I only wear gloves while spraying coats of paint in the booth or cleaning my equipment. All other times I am barehanded, which can cause strange fingerprints to appear under the clear coat months later. It is amazing the crap that gets caught in the ridges of fingerprints.

I must wash my hands every 20 minutes when I'm laying out tape, as in taping off flames or graphics. I wash up each time before I wet sand. I'm not as picky when I spend my time airbrushing, as I don't touch the surface much with my fingers. But then again, I don't airbrush with fried-chicken grease-slathered hands, either. It's when my hands are touching the painted surface that I try to keep them totally free of any oils. Hands also pick up oils from touching skin. I keep a long-handled artist's paintbrush near my workbench to use as an itch scratcher. I always keep cotton swabs around to clean my airbrushes, and they work great for little ear itches. In the winter, all that washing can be a little hard on the hands, but it's harder on your nerves when tape pulls loose because it was laid over an oily spot. It's even more stressful finding the whitish glow of a nice, neat fingerprint against what you thought was a flawless black surface. I also use a clean washcloth to hold onto the parts while I am wet sanding them. When handling dry parts, I use paper towels between my hands and the painted surface. My skin very seldom touches a wet or ready-to-spray painted surface. See fig. 3. I use mounting areas to hold parts, like the tank mounts or the bottoms and cutouts in fenders. I have learned too many hard lessons in this area.

Rule Number 7. *Try not to paint custom colors on cloudy days.* Yet in many cases, nighttime painting is the only option. *If you have a lot of evenly distributed light in your painting area, you can paint any time.* I only mention this because this is just another way to reduce painting errors. I try not to spray any color on anything but a sunny day. Reason? After the paint is dry to the touch, I take one part, usually the front fender—handling it very carefully from the bottom—out into the sun to check it. If I'm painting black, for example, I'll be able to tell if any little bits of pearl or metallic from a previous job have landed in the paint. With custom colors, I check the part against the color sample I made, seeing if the color is correct or if I need another coat of paint. I've tried this with electric natural lights, portable halogens, and all kinds of artificial light, only to find later on that I needed to do things differently after I saw the parts in direct sunlight. So now I don't take chances. I try to wait for a sunny day, no matter how much the customer is yowling. They howl louder once their buddies start pointing out inconsistencies in their paint.

To make matters more difficult, any flaw or defect that doesn't show up in the direct sunlight will show up on cloudy days, especially color banding from improperly applied pearl paint or too few coats of pearl. So before doing artwork over your base coat, to know for certain that it is correct, check it in sunlight, indirect light, and artificial light, as most indoor bike shows will have that kind of light. (Beware, because when the color looks great in the booth light, chances are if you look at it in the direct sunlight, you'll find you need to apply one more coat.) My painting buddies tease me about this, but for me it's worth the effort.

Rule Number 8. *Read through each chapter completely before you try using the process it details.* This is not a painting rule, but good common sense for using this book. You wouldn't jump out of an airplane before you've finished reading the parachute instructions, would you? Underline or mark parts that you want to really remember when using the process. And if boo-boos crop up, don't panic, don't freak out—just calmly research the problem by reading the tech sheet on the product you are using and checking the chapter that deals with that process and the troubleshooting chapter. And don't be afraid to ask the opinions of other painters. Chances are they have been there and know a little trick that will save you.

EQUIPMENT

Start with substandard equipment and chances are you're going to get a substandard paint job. Those paint guns I threw against the wall 25 years ago? They were all cheapo guns or used-to-death stuff that should have hit the trash heap long before I got to it. Good quality paint guns and filtering equipment is money well spent. With proper care, quality equipment will last many, many years. Although my absolute preference is the Mini Sata Jet, and following that, most of the Sata line of equipment, most top-of-the-line spray-gun manufacturers make guns and equipment that will do the work for you just as well.

SPRAY GUNS

Quality equipment is expensive. But you have to ask yourself, "Is it worth it?" Put it this way: You're standing there, the cheapo gun or gun that you borrowed from your pop-in-law who used to paint in your hand, staring at that blob that just came out of the nozzle that has ruined that perfect coat of candy apple paint you were admiring just a moment ago. You've just set yourself back by a day, not counting the wasted material. Or suddenly the airflow or the paint flow ain't flowing the way it was yesterday, or even a moment ago. Now you've got to stop, pour out the paint, pull the gun apart, looking for the cause of the problem. You could have been done, cleaned up, and leaving for a beer. Instead you're spending time dealing with an unnecessary problem. Can't afford that gun? How much is your time worth? When a paint job goes bad from a cheap gun, you'll give anything to turn back the clock and use a quality spray gun. With the obscenely high cost of paint and painting materials, can you afford *not* to use a good spray gun?

Sata makes the perfect guns for any kind of painting, especially motorcycle painting. From the top-of-the-line Satajet 2000 HVLP Digital 2 to the RP Digital. See fig. 4. The RP's heavy spray is perfect for clear coating. With the digital readout right on the handle, the painter can perfectly dial in the optimum air pressure.

I used to use old junk guns for priming, and I paid the price in extra time sanding. A uniformly applied round of primer will save time in the sanding phase and provide a smoother surface for color coating. Don't skimp, even on a primer gun. See fig. 5.

My favorite treasure from Sata is the Mini Jet 3 HVLP gun. See fig. 6. It is the perfect spray gun for bike painting. It uses low pressure, which means even if your spray booth isn't immaculate, you won't be blowing dirty dust onto the wet paint surface. With its tight spray pattern and low pressure, it uses less material. Nozzle sizes range from 0.3 to 1.2, the latter being what I use. It also comes in a kit with individual bottles that turn the gun into a big airbrush, making quick color changes a snap. If I could only use one gun in my shop, it would be the Mini Jet 3. It is the most important piece of equipment in my paint shop. Sata has just released the Mini Jet 4; the next generation of Mini guns.

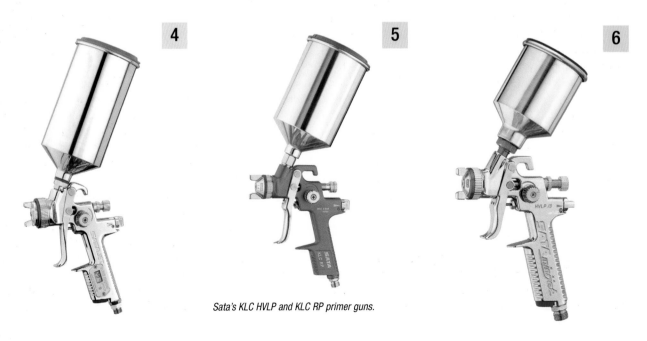

Sata's KLC HVLP and KLC RP primer guns.

7

with a 25-gallon tank. It provided plenty of air pressure and plugged into a standard 110 outlet. It's also small enough to move around easily. Painting cars and using air tools like grinders and sanders can drain down the tank quickly, but for overall bike painting and airbrushing needs, it can be the way to go. An even better choice is a 7.5- to 10-horsepower, two-stage air compressor, especially if you're using HVLP spray guns.

8

FILTERING EQUIPMENT

It's no good having premium guns and using high-buck paint if the air going through the gun and carrying the paint onto the surface is dirty. I've seen crap blow out of guns that had all kinds of air dryers and such in the system. You take a look the next morning and see problems, and after wasting a morning or a day chasing down the cause, you find it could have been avoided if only you'd used the proper equipment—I've learned that lesson too many times. At the very least, get a good quality water separator. But you really need a quality filtering system right in your booth, or at least no more than 50 feet away from the gun. Sata's 0/444 modular system of lined up filters makes it easy. See fig. 7. The first filter precleans down to 5 microns. The second stage filter goes down to 0.01 microns. The setup even includes two outlets, one for your gun hose and one for an air-supplied respirator. (I'll elaborate more on that in the safety section.) Why spend money to take so many precautions? Like I said, time is money—the horrible thing is, chances are you won't know something has gone wrong until the last coat has been sprayed.

AIR COMPRESSORS

Over the years, I have found that if you're doing anything other than light airbrushing—that is using spray guns—it is best to have a compressor with a storage tank. For many years, I used a five-horsepower, single-cylinder compressor

PAINT STANDS

It seems everyone asks me about paint stands for bike parts. I am lucky enough to have friends who fabricated and welded a few stands for me. (Thanks, Jeff O!) My fender stand is basically a large-diameter pipe set into a heavy base with a strip of heavy-duty sheet metal bent in the shape of a fender, welded to the top. See fig. 8.

For tanks, I use a fixture made of heavy-duty, threaded rod with a "T" pipe fitting at one end and bent up at the other. See fig. 9. The bottom of the "T" is threaded into a piece of pipe that fits into the end of a bushing set into the top of the large diameter pipe. See fig. 10. While the stands I use are pretty specialized, I know folks who have made paint stands out of two-by-fours. If I have a part that's hard to set up, like an oil tank or airdam, I play around with wire

or fabricate fixtures to rig onto my paint stands. Sometimes I'll run a pipe from one fender stand to the other, using 2-inch masking tape to hold it in place, then I'll hang parts from that. I'll prop parts onto papered-off, plastic filler cans set on tables. It pays to be creative; there's no limit to what you can use. But I always use masking paper to tape off everything. And if it looks like a part is not too secure on the stand, I use 2-inch masking tape to secure it. With fender stands, roll a piece of tape in a circle so the sticky part is on

the outside and stick a few of those to the place where the stand touches inside of the fender. And always double-check to make sure your parts are secure on the stand. If you have any doubts, gently wiggle the stand with the part on it. You don't want to come back into the paint booth to see beautifully painted parts lying dented on the floor. (I've made some incredible saves as parts fell to the floor, but there were a few victims.) And pay attention to that air hose. Your attention may be so focused on spraying that coat of candy, you won't notice that the hose has wrapped around a stand and is about to tip it over. My next book will show extensively how to make paint stands.

HANGING FRAMES

That book will also show exactly how to hang a frame and swingarm. But here's a quick explanation: I use eyehooks to hang chains from the ceiling. The rear chain hangs down and each end loops around a long metal rod that runs through either the rear axle mounts on a rigid frame or through the rear fender mounts on a softail frame. See fig. 11.

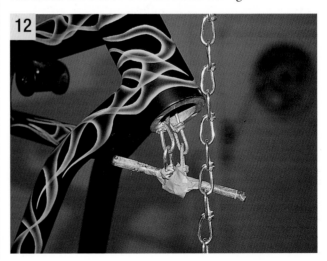

The front chain loops down through the neck, where I run a small metal rod through the chain, secured with tape. See fig. 12. Always try to start at the same place on the frame, then work your way around, following a pattern. Always make sure the frame is hung high enough to spray under it, but not high enough to miss spots on the neck and backbone.

SAVE THE FRAME'S VIN NUMBER

The most common frame painting error is painting over and obscuring the frame's identification number. Sometimes the numbers are not very deeply etched. They'll need to be scribed out with a pick after each round of paint. In extreme cases, the numbers are taped off before each round of paint, and never receive the same depth of paint as the rest of the frame. DMV inspectors will readily reject any bike with hard to read frame numbers. Before any paint is applied, find the VIN number and cover it with masking tape. Trim the tape so it makes a neat "frame" around the number. Then spray the primer coats. Remove the tape before the last coat and spray a light coat of primer over the numbers. Then do this with the base and clear coats. I try to make the color difference hard to notice, but it will be different. Trust me, it is better to have a small, neat rectangular area of a slightly different color than to have to dig out those numbers from 11 layers of paint.

13

SAFETY

Try not to store paint in the basement of your home or in an attached garage. All those fumes are a horrible fire and health hazard. It just takes one spark. I store my paint in a detached shed. And never do overall spray work in the basement or a spare room—a very bad idea. If you'll be airbrushing in your home, make sure you have excellent ventilation. More on that in Chapter 5.

Look at that vibrant girl. See fig. 13. Looks pretty healthy, doesn't she? Unfortunately she looked a whole lot better on the outside than the inside. She's me, and I painted for years and didn't use a fresh-air-supplied respirator. Painters don't die of old age. I was slowly poisoning myself.

I want as many years as I can get. For years, I had been thinking about getting a fresh air system. But I always had an excuse: too expensive, too bulky, dragging around all those hoses. But one morning, after spending an entire day in the booth, I woke up feeling like crap. I felt like I had food poisoning, and I knew why. This had happened many times before, but I always shrugged it off and toughed it out. Being tough is being there to provide for your family—coughing and dying young because you were stubborn is *not* tough.

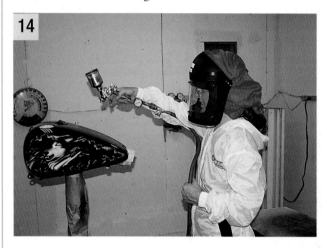
14

So when Sata came out with its new fresh air system, I had no more excuses. One hose to supply air, quick and easy disconnects from the small carbon filter belt unit, and a very lightweight helmet. The system uses replaceable tear-off sheets for the visor with no separate compressor and no heavy hoses dragging around. I'm through with waking up sick.

I'll be nervous about all those isosynants I inhaled through my traditional respirator for the rest of my life. If I could go back in time and use a fresh air system, I would. I'd pay whatever price to not risk shortening my life. Don't take chances. Go get that respirator. For the price of a full set of riding leathers, it's well worth it. Life is way, way too short as it is.

I also wear a paint suit in the booth, and gloves. See fig. 14. I never let any solvents get on my skin. If they do, I dry them off immediately. If I get paint on my skin, I use a product like 3M's Paint Buster to wash it off. I never use thinner or reducer to wash my hands. (Further on in this book there's a good story about a buddy of mine who used to take lacquer thinner baths.) Avoid at all costs breathing the chemicals used for cleaning a spray gun—they will kill you. OK, I'm done preaching and its time to get to the fun parts.

THE GREAT GAS CAP OPENING CONTROVERSY

Ever since motorcycle companies thought up the idea of screw-in gas caps, there have been problems related to paint adhesion around that area. My method of prepping that area is simple. I very thoroughly sand that area, going right up to the outer ring of the opening. I tape off the ring each time I paint, and remove the tape after sanding, keeping the paint edge clean and low. Don't allow the paint edge over that ring. If you do, the fumes from the gasoline will work at the edge and sneak under it, and lift the paint. See fig. 15.

For older bikes that have only a smooth-edged opening and no outer ring, tape off the hole halfway up the edge of the opening. See fig. 16. Retape and resand each time you paint. Then seal down the paint edge using a good quality, clear fingernail polish. Don't scoff—I've used this trick for years, and it works.

BEWARE OF TOO-THICK PAINT

The insane compromise of custom paint on bikes is that in numerous cases, many layers of paint will have to be applied to get the perfect color. It becomes a problem when parts bolt against heavily layered surfaces, squash down the paint, and cause it to lift and bubble. The problem areas tend to be around seat mounting holes on rear fenders, fender-mounting holes on softail frames, and the mounting holes on front fenders and tanks.

The remedy is to know where parts will bolt against what you're painting. Try to keep the paint in those areas as thin as possible, and that includes primer. And always make sure to sand those areas thoroughly, so the paint will stick well. With some colors, like candy, it is impossible to only lightly spray certain areas, as the color needs to be evenly distributed. But primer and clear coats can still be manipulated to accommodate problem areas.

Watch out for paint piling up on the edges of fenders. Sand off any excess material.

BEFORE YOU PAINT

Before you start any paint job, check your parts. Make sure they're the right ones, especially if the customer ordered new parts and brought them to you. If you ordered them, double-check to see that they are correct parts for the bike. If you don't, you may end up in a situation demonstrated by the tanks above. See fig. 17. The customer had a fuel-injected bike. The dealer ordered a tank for a carbureted bike. The dealer also ordered a front fender for a springer, when the bike had a conventional front end. I whipped up a killer paint job and e-mailed the owner pictures, but no one caught the mistakes until weeks after the parts arrived at the dealer. The parts didn't fit. Ouch! (Well, ouch for dealer anyway.) It is not as big of a problem for me, because I get paid to do it all over again. But it was not fun trying to perfectly duplicate a very distinctive skull. This happens more often than you think. Every time I order parts, I double-check three times: after I order them, before I pay for them, and after they arrive.

This book deals with acrylic urethane base coats and urethane clear enamels, not lacquer. Although there are painters who still work exclusively with lacquer, I no longer use it. I used to swear by it, at one time, and couldn't imagine using anything else. But when lacquers started getting hard to find, I switched over to the urethane enamels. I airbrush with base coat enamel, but all my primers, candy, and clear coats are done in two-part. I use a two-part primer like PPG's K36 Prima hardened with K201, mixed 5:1; add a dribble of DT reducer, and you're ready to paint over sandblasted metal. Some painters use an etching priming before they apply the filler primer. I never paint over bare metal that has not been sandblasted. Paint needs a good "tooth" to bite to. Parts that come as bare metal often have an oily coating, so wash the metal down with lacquer thinner first, then sandblast the parts. Make sure all openings on gas tanks and oil tanks are stuffed with paper towels and sealed with duct tape so sand doesn't get inside. For spraying over existing paint, wash down the surface with a strong precleaner until it squeaks, and then wet sand it with 220-grit sandpaper. Next, apply two-part epoxy primer and then two-part primer over the paint surface.

PREPPING FIBERGLASS AND PLASTIC PARTS

Never sandblast plastic or fiberglass parts! For parts like hard saddlebags, sidecovers, fairings, and such, wet sand them down with 320 grit, or media blast, which will not leave the fuzz on plastic that sanding does. I like to wet sand whenever possible for the smooth surface that it leaves. Sand scratches can be a real problem with fiberglass or hard plastic parts, so I try to get a good tooth on the surface but not end up with deep scratches that will come back to haunt me through five coats of previously flawless candy paint. Once sanded, parts are ready for epoxy primer and base coat color. For certain parts that have a slight flex to them like polypropylene, you'll need to use a special clear primer made specifically those parts. Any brand of paint system will have a product for painting flexible or black plastic parts. Dust two coats of that on, then apply your two-part primers.

After applying and sanding primer coats and just before spraying color coats, I spray on a quick-drying, three-part epoxy sealer. PPG's DP50LF consists of two parts epoxy primer, one part catalyst (DP402LF), and one-half part reducer (DT reducer.) The primers for PPG's epoxy sealer come in five colors, designated by a two-digit number. This seals the surface in case there are sand-throughs down to the metal or through the various layers of primer. It also helps to smooth over any deep sanding scratches. Now you're ready for color coats.

CHAPTER 2
FOOLPROOF BASE COAT PAINTING

It took me 12 hours to do this four-color candy fade. I had never tried anything like this.

This will be a short chapter, because I've already gone over the rules. And once you apply common sense to your painting methods, you take most of the guesswork out of it. Always read the product sheets on the paint product you are using. They'll recommend things like how many coats should be applied, the overlap of coats you'll need, air pressures, and how long to wait between coats. If you didn't get a product sheet when you bought your paint, go online and see if you can download one from the company's website. And try to also read the MSDS sheets as well, which will tell you about the product you are using, compound contents, and safety. MSDS sheets sometimes also tell you what the product plays well with, or doesn't. And ask your paint dealer regularly if there are updates. Even if you've been painting for years, when

you run into a problem and need a quick answer, that tech info can come in very, very handy.

My method of laying down coats of paint is simple. I spray one coat in one direction, say horizontally. Then I run the next coat up and down, vertically. The following coat I'll run diagonally. This is the best way to get total coverage with no color bands—lines of darker color running through the job. It doesn't tend to be a big problem with solid, nonmetallic colors, but with pearl or candy colors it can be a pesky problem, especially if there aren't enough coats of paint. A future book will go over the basic painting process inside, outside, and upside-down for all kinds of paint, but the focus of this book is on custom artwork techniques, so I'll only cover the barest basics.

THE TWO-GUN SOLUTION

Try to have at least two spray guns to use: one for primer, pearls, most solid colors, and metallics, and the other for black, white, candy, and clear. It's better yet to have three guns—a separate gun for primer. If you can only afford one gun, you'll have to keep it super clean, as bits of pearl and primer get stuck in the gun and then make an appearance the next time black is sprayed. I use cotton swabs to wipe out the interior of the gun after the head and needle are removed and wiped clean. Better to have to more than one gun if you are painting more than one bike at a time on a regular basis. I have a primer gun, one for pearls/metallics, one for solid colors, a candy/black gun, and a clear coat gun.

HOK Snowwhite Pearl white gives an icy glow to this simple artwork

BASE COAT COLORS

I carefully choose only base coat colors that will complement the artwork I'll be doing. First, I like to look through paint books and find interesting colors. Then I talk a customer into using one of them. I've gotten some strange looks over the colors I pick, but every time I get to use some funky color, the result is perfect. Whatever color you choose, it is a good idea to keep track of what you use and the number of coats you apply. Keep a file for every paint job and try to put as much information on that paint job as you can. Even if you just scrawl on a cocktail napkin, "3 coats silver base, 5 coats blue candy, clear mixed with concentrate med dark" and stick it in a folder, this information can come back to help you in the future. I usually make these notes when I'm making my sample piece.

And keep in mind the temperature of the parts you're painting. If the parts were just removed from a colder section of the shop and your booth or spray area is warmer, give the parts time to heat up. Painting cold parts in a warm area with warm paint can result in crazing or cracking.

PEARL COLORS

This quick step-by-step outlines a pearl paint application. Undercoat painting can determine the intensity of the finished product. Are you looking for a dark base coat that's almost black, but want the color to light up where the sunlight hits it? Go with a black undercoat, and then dust a bit of pearl on the parts. Try to use the same color pearl as the end-result color, for example, purple pearl for a purple-tinted color. Then follow that with a few coats of candy in the end result color. Keep in mind that the more pearl you use, the brighter the color will be. Don't use too much candy, as the more pearl and candy you use, the less black it will be. Another trick is to mix pearl into solid colors, such as red, and use that as a base, then layer a few coats of candy over it.

HOK Red KF-01 to Gold Kameleon color. *Aaron Stevenson*

Color-changing pearl paint is also applied over a black base coat for its most dramatic effect. **See fig. 3.** I find that three to four medium coats are all I need to spray. Always use a wide gun pattern to spray pearls or metallics, and don't go too dry with your coats. Lay them on smooth and flat. If your gun is spraying too dry or you're holding the gun too far away, you'll get a bumpy, hairy surface to the pearl, and you'll lose that endless depth effect that you want. If you do see a bumpy surface building up, stop painting. Let it dry overnight, wet sand with 600 grit, then start over by repainting the black or white undercoat. If this is your first time spraying pearls, experiment on a test panel first. Paint is horribly expensive these days, so play it safe. Get used to the material. Waste a little on a test panel instead of a lot on a whole set of sheet metal.

Here I used a white undercoat to really make the pearl glow. **See fig. 4.** White undercoats can also make regular solid colors (like reds or blues) glow. Whenever I spray yellow, I always use a white undercoat. For this application I wanted a bright, rich blue.

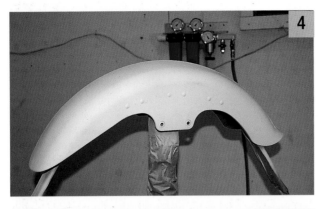

Again, I changed the direction I moved the paint gun each time I laid on a coat of paint, and used a wide gun pattern.

Always make sure there is plenty of light in the paint booth. In order to get even coverage when painting, look over the part to find a reflection of light on the surface being painted. Watch the flow as the paint hits the surface and move the gun accordingly. I never make a final decision on the number of coats or on my final color without taking a break away from the booth. Once you think you're done, go have lunch, clear your head, and then recheck your color. (This is why you need to know your material—the product sheet will tell you how much time you have between coats or to recoat without resanding.)

Before the blue candy was applied.

This was a color I'd been wanting to use for a while, HOK UK-02 Lime Gold Candy.

So I went with House of Kolor's PBC 36 True Blue Pearl Shimrin and put a few coats of clear over the True Blue, which was tinted slightly with HOK's KK-04 Oriental Blue Kandy Koncentrate. **See fig. 5.**

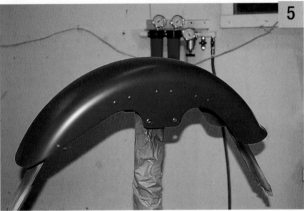

The finished color. The graphics colors help accent the blue base.

I simply drizzle a little of the concentrate toner into the already mixed clear. Other companies also make toners that can be mixed with clear. With extensive knowledge of the paint system being used, you can really play around to create your own custom colors.

CANDY COLORS

Candy color application is much like the pearl application, except that instead of clear coat after the pearl, candy color is used. Also, metallic undercoats for candy are usually brighter than pearl, so they can reflect through the candy. Many paint companies are getting into the custom color game, with many choices of differently colored undercoats for candy paint: the usual silver and gold, but also tones of blue, green, purple, and many others. House of Kolor (HOK) pioneered this system and makes creating custom colors a breeze. With so many bases and the endless candy choices, you can get really wild.

But there are as many debates on the best way to apply candy as there are choices of color combos. Some painters insist the only way to spray candy is with factory-mixed candy urethane. Others prefer to mix candy concentrate or toner in base coat or urethane clear. Find what method and material works best for you. I like to use my favorite urethane clear and mix candy concentrate into it. That way I can totally play with the intensity of the candy tones, the way I did in the above example over the pearl blue.

I usually start out with lighter coats of candy, getting a nice even application of color. Once I have two light to medium coats applied, then I add a bit more concentrate to my clear mix. As to how much concentrate to mix in the clear, I just do it by eye, but

I always mix my paint in plastic cups with measurements on them, like E-Z Mix plastic cups. Other painters swear by using the measurements on a metal paint paddle. After you mix up the candy, stir it with a paint stick and check the intensity of the color by looking at the stick. It's better to go too light than too dark. If the color is too dark, you'll end up with a stripe effect—not good. When mixing candies for strength or certain effects, use either a stainless steel or aluminum paddle, so you have a constant color base to look at. And try not to paint candy on a cloudy day, especially if you are a new painter. Judging the paint in the sunlight is essential. Also take care not to run the paint around the edges of the fenders, causing a ridge on the fender edge.

Classic HOK Candy Apple Red UK-11.

PAINTING FRAMES AND SWINGARMS

If there was ever a bike component on which a mini paint gun was meant to be used, it is a bike frame. Mini guns have made frame painting much less of a hassle for me. The tighter spray pattern control of a mini gun will keep the paint aimed on the frame—not as much will be lost in the air—and better control means less chance for runs and sags. Also, the smaller gun tends to fit into tight spaces better, which is critical for some frames. You'll use much less paint and obtain better results. Have a plan when painting frames. Find a point to start at and plan a pattern that will be followed with each coat, working your way around the frame, finding the most effective paint spray direction. Spray at 45-degree angles to your eye, so that your overlap will be even. When painting tubing, use a moderate fan pattern on a little gun, paint longitudinally ("with" a tube), *never* across, and paint the underside of the frame first.

Candy application can be a challenge, as dark spots can form as the frame is painted from many angles. Solid colors tend to show coverage better, but it is not as easy to see coverage with candy. Look over the frame for problems before each coat. When painting frames, swingarms, and any other parts, places like the bottom of the frame rails or edges of the fenders, always get less color coverage—but it seems to really be a problem on frames and swingarms. The foolproof way I have for dealing with this is simple.

When I think I'm done with my color coats, I shine a flashlight over and under the frame to find any light spots that need more color. **See fig. 9.** It never fails—I always find a place where the color is thin. Here you can see the flashlight focusing on the neck.

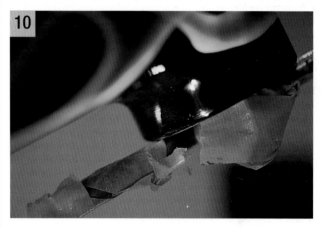

See where the paint is thin? The light spots are easy to see. These are nearly invisible in regular light. **See fig. 10.**

Notice the thin paint spot along the edge of the rear axle mount—another flaw that wouldn't show until the bike is in the sun. **See fig. 11.**

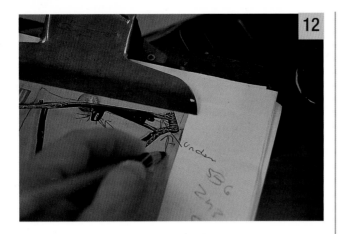

Next, I take a digital photo or create a stick-figure drawing of the frame and mark on the photo or drawing where I need to make the touchups. **See fig. 12.** I don't even try to remember them all. After the paint is dry, I examine and document problems again. I also sometimes find these areas when I am about to wet sand. I just keep my clipboard close by and make notes, going over the parts before sanding, turning them over, and inspecting them. To spray colors on these light areas after wet sanding, I use an airbrush or a mini spray gun with the pattern narrowed and fluid and air controls turned way down.

I do a lot of artwork on black frames, and take many precautions to keep that black clean. It's an even better idea to replace your frame-hanging chains regularly. So the best trick for painting frames is a very simple one: Have two sets of frame-hanging chains—one for pearl, metallic base, candy, and solid-color coats, and one for black and clear coats. The problem is that dust or debris from the previous coats can break loose and land on the black or clear.

CLEAR COATS

After spraying any color, always apply a few coats of clear, intercoat, base coat, or urethane. This protects your base and gives you the surface you'll need to sand, once you're ready for more coats or artwork. At this point, if no artwork is going over the base paint, you may be able to get away with doing your finish clear coats. I recommend—as does my clear coat painter, Wayne Springs of Little Rock Auto Body—wet sanding the clear coats with 600- or 800-grit paper anyway. Don't overdo it and go through the clear to the color coats, just give the surface a smooth scuffdown so no shiny areas are visible. Then do your finish clear. Chapter 15 offers further instructions.

White undercoats will brighten up any base color. This photo shows what can be happen when playing around with colors and design. I achieved this wild purple color by first laying down a white base, then layering on HOK Violette Candy UK-17. The liquid graphic shaded with purple candy (HOK Wild Cherry KK-3 mixed 1:1 with HOK Cobalt Blue KK-5) adds even more dimension to the base color. Be careful when spraying candy over a solid white base. Specks of dust that land in the candy will show up as dark spots that are really noticeable. I only used white for the base coat here because I really needed the purple to glow, and I knew I would cover it with the webbing so little flaws wouldn't show. The little evil skull peeking through is small but very effective.

CHAPTER 3
FLAKING OUT—
PAINTING FLAKE COLORS

MATERIAL AND EQUIPMENT

- House of Kolor F-20 red flake
- Course metallic base coat color which is same tone as flake
- House of Kolor K-01 Brandywine Kandy Koncentrate
- Base coat Clear
- Urethane Clear
- Reducer
- Sata K3 RP Digital
- Sata Agitator cup
- Sata Mini Jet 3
- HOK Flake spoon

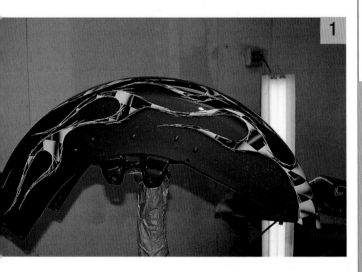

1

Back in the 1960s and 1970s, flake paint was very popular. It was everywhere, on vans, cars, speedboats, and especially bikes. It slowly faded away, but in the new century folks are rediscovering flake paint and its endless possibilities. I like House of Kolor's line of flake. The colors are vibrant, and while the flake is brilliant, it's thin and lays down flat, requiring less clear to level out the surface. The two biggest problems with painting flake colors are the mess that results from the application and the rough surface of the freshly applied flake paint, which in turn requires tons of clear coat. I use a few tricks to make the flake process painless—well, sort of painless.

I'll address the last problem first. I try to never spray flake in my paint booth. The flakes are heavier than metallics and pearl colors and tend to land everywhere. The floor will be covered with them and they'll try to get into every coat of paint you spray for months afterward. I try to spray flake outside, where the flakes will land on the ground and stay out of the booth. Of course, the weather and environmental laws don't always allow for that.

For the paint job I used in this chapter, time was short. The customer needed his bike for Daytona Bike Week. I did not have the luxury of waiting for a sunny day. It was a damp, cloudy day that was getting dark by the time I was ready to spray. I had no choice but to spray the flake in the booth, then spend a few hours cleaning the booth the following day. To clean up from flake, first grab the shop vac and suck up everything on the floor and any cobwebs that might have gathered in the corners. Then sweep with a soft-bristled broom, carefully looking to see how much flake is still there. The next step is mopping the floor, again looking to see how much flake remains. Flake will come back to haunt you if you don't get it all up—treat it like nuclear waste and save yourself headaches in the future.

HANDY HINT
Make a sample before you paint your parts. For this job, the customer wasn't 100 percent sure he wanted the aggressive look of a flake finish. So I made up three samples, two with HOK F-20 Red Flake and one painted with HOK's MBC Pale Gold Base, which has a slightly finer flake than the regular flake. All samples were then coated with HOK Brandywine Kandy Koncentrate mixed with HOK's Intercoat Clear. Half of each sample had four coats of candy, the other half had six coats. The customer had six samples to choose from, and happily went with the F-20 red flake with four coats of candy. It was a medium bright red, very brilliant.

Spray a black base coat. **See fig. 2.** Here's the main trick: Get out the coarsest base coat silver you have. If you are applying a gold flake, use the coarsest gold metallic available. If using a silver or colored flake, try HOK Orion Silver Shimrin BC-01. If going with a colored flake, find the toner or dye that goes best with the colored flake. In this example, I'm using HOK F-20 flake. KK-01- Kandy Brandywine Koncentrate, is very close in tone to the F-20. So I'll lay down a coarse red metallic base.

2

3

5

I take the KK-01 and mix a small amount in some BC-01, creating a red-toned metallic base coat that comes very close to the flake color. See fig. 3.

The biggest challenge to applying flake is obtaining good coverage. The more layers of flake you apply, the rougher the surface will be and the more coats of clear will be necessary to smooth it out. Too many clear coats are *not* a good thing. So by using the metallic base under the flake coats, it won't take as much flake to cover the surface. All those spaces between the flakes won't be noticeable. HOK advises painters to not use more than three coats of flake, or lots of clear coating will be needed.

Apply two to three coats of the metallic base coat over the black base. **See fig. 4.**

Next, mix up the flake. To spray F-20 flake, HOK recommends mixing two level teaspoons (one ounce) of flake for every quart of mixed clear coat. See fig. 5. HOK makes a neat little adjustable spoon to precisely measure out the amount of flake you need. You can use most any kind of clear with your flake. In this instance I used HOK Intercoat Clear mixed 2:1 with reducer.

I used a Sata RP spray gun with a Sata Agitator mixing cup. **See fig. 6.** The Sata cup has a paddle that uses air to propel it and keep the flake mixed—with the gravity-feed guns, the flake has a tendency to settle in the gun's paint chamber. If you use a gravity feed and suspect this is happening, hold a bundled rag over the gun

4

6

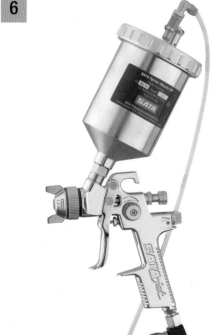

nozzle and pull the trigger. It will force air through the paint chamber and into the cup, clearing out any clogging flakes. This trick can be used to keep the flake mixed in the cup, if you don't use an agitator cup. Just give it a zap before applying each coat, but be sure not to blow the lid off the gun if it's a snap-on lid.

Now adjust the gun and lay down the first coat of flake using a 50 percent pattern overlap. This means laying down one pass with the spray gun, then on the next pass covering half of the first pass with the second. So if the second pass is laid down under the first, the bottom half of the first pass will be covered by the second pass. The third pass will cover the bottom half of the second pass and so on. Hold the gun about six inches from the surface of the part—any farther and the surface will be too rough.

7

Three coats of flake works just fine, but for a truly wild flake layer, you may want to play with four or five coats. Spray the flakes close to the surface, trying to lay them flat to reflect more light. **See fig. 7.** Check the surface before you apply each coat to see if it is getting a rough, hairy feel. If the surface is starting to feel rough, there are several things that can be done. One is to mix more clear in the flake, then flood on a heavy coat, but not heavy enough to run. What you're trying to do is smooth out the surface.

Or if the surface is extremely rough, stop spraying flake and apply a few layers of clear until the surface is smoother. Then let it dry. Lightly wet sand with 600 grit the next day. Remember not to sand too hard and go through the clear coat into the flake coat. Then apply the rest of the flake coats. Check *before* each coat. Your head will be clearer and the surface sort of dry, so you can actually feel it to see just how rough it is. Use common sense as you go—balance your desire to be flaky with your desire for a good clear coat. If it is not too rough after your last flake coat, step back and dust a dry coat on, standing a few flakes up. Do *not* overdo this.

HANDY HINT

When finished with the HOK measuring spoon, store it in a plastic bag. It has bits of flake all over it. Rinse it off the best you can, then store in bag. This way, whenever you touch it and you're *not* spraying flake, you won't contaminate your hands and get flakes in what was supposed to be a spotless coat of pure white.

Now all the flake coats are applied. If you're using urethane clear to apply the flake, move right onto the next step. I used Intercoat Clear, so I waited until it had dried a bit. I used the base coat clear because it isn't as thick as urethane and it dries faster. I waited about a half hour, enough time to grab some supper and clear my head.

HANDY HINT

Time spent in the spray booth can make things murky without you realizing it. You can be staring straight at a problem and not see it. Taking time away from the booth and literally airing out your system will help your senses. After time away from the booth, step back in to check out your work. 5 out of 10 times, you'll see something that you missed or something you need to fix before you proceed. I used a Sata Air Supplied system, but I still took a little break before proceeding.

8

If you want to apply some candy color over the flake, mix up some clear (either urethane, referred to as "uro," or base coat, whatever was used to apply the flake) and mix in candy concentrate or dye. I used the HOK KK-01. If no color is needed, just skip ahead to the clear coat process. I use less color for the first two coats, and layer it on very evenly. Then I put in more toner and get a "darker" clear color. In this example I put on four coats of candy. **See fig. 8.**

HANDY HINT

Know your clear. There are some clears that won't allow you to apply as many coats of clear as I am using in this example. I can layer on as many as 6-7 coats of clear and get away with it. But I know my clear. I've been using it for 8 years. I trust it. Know the products you use. Test them, abuse them, see just how far you can push them. Know their limits.

CLEARING

Now you've got flake layers, and maybe color layers, applied. It's time to hit the existing layers with your favorite filling clear. Fill with three to four coats if you did not use any candy over your flake, or two coats if you did. Some painters recommend going straight to the clear color process and leaving the candy color application for a later time. If you go that route, apply the flake layers and then apply three to four coats of clear urethane or base coat.

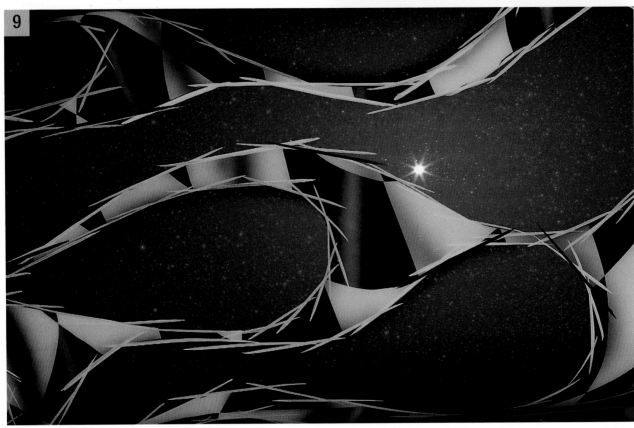

For the clear coat process, wet sand clear coated flake layers with 600 grit, being careful not to sand too much and break through any flakes or the flake layers. If you get any light spots in candy flake jobs, retouch carefully with candy.

Either way, once you've got the flake and/or color coats under the first round of clear, the job should only require one more round of three to four clear coats, and you're good to go. Artwork or finishing clear coat can now be applied. Depending on the amount of paint laid on, it can take up to 30 days for the paint to dry enough so the flakes don't poke through the finish, as the clear dries around it. But most of the time I wait a week or even less.

Here's a close-up of the flake with the candy over it. I airbrushed a wild checkered flame design over it. The flake base paint really makes this paint job pop. **Figs. 9, 10, and 11.**

CHAPTER 4
MARBLIZED BASE COAT PAINTING

MATERIAL AND EQUIPMENT

- House of Kolor MB-01 Silverwhite Marblizer
- House of Kolor MB-00 Neutral Marblizer
- Black base coat
- Any color candy paint (if applicable)
- Base coat or Urethane clear
- House of Kolor Intercoat Clear SG-100
- Reducer
- Shiny masking paper
- Masking tape
- Plastic wrap or any odd non-cloth material
- Sata Mini Jet 1.2 nozzle 1 for marblizer
- Sata Mini Jet 1.2 nozzle 1 for black, candy, and clear coats

It is important to use a separate mini gun for the marblizing application.

Everyone who has seen the paint in the picture above asks me how I did it. Very simply, I broke the rules for painting Marblizer. Marblizer isn't supposed to work if used the way I used it. And it's certainly not supposed to last. I painted this bike for Sturgis 2002. Two years and many miles later, it still looks great.

It was absolute hell figuring out how to make this method work, though. The first few tries failed miserably—bubbling and lifting all over, the candy separating from the Marblizer base paint. It was horrible. But what had mystified me was that the test piece had been a total success. I could have left tape to sit on that test part for a week and it wouldn't have lifted the paint when removed.

Then I realized the problem. I always abuse my test pieces, flooding on layers of paint, trying to make the paint screw up. I had been *too* careful. It was July 4 weekend, 2002. Sturgis was less than a month away, and we had already repainted the bike from scratch. When I went to pick up the parts to do the artwork, I saw the bubbles. Another failure. It was Wednesday. My helpers were ready to take off for the holiday weekend and wanted no part of this hopeless project: "We'll get on it first thing Monday." My answer to them was, "This thing will be in the shop, going together on Monday." They laughed at me and I drove off with the parts. I went straight to the sandblaster, who looked at the soft paint and said, "We're better off peeling this thing like a banana." So for five hours, the crew at Vintage Cars, including a couple of retired guys who had the misfortune of being there that day, and I peeled a frame, swingarm, gas tank, and two full fenders right down the primer using razor blades. Next, I brought the pile home and put my neighbor and her son to work sanding with 80 grit paper. The parts were back in primer that night. I finally shut down the booth at 5 a.m. and Thursday, got to work sanding primer and putting the parts in black and Marblizer. It was hell in that booth.

There was no time for another failed attempt. I was almost sure I had figured out the problem, but my hand still shook as I sprayed the final urethane coats at 3 a.m. On Friday, I layered on the candy tangerine and clear. My husband took the frame and swingarm into work Saturday morning to start the assembly. I did the graphics over the next three days and the bike made it to Sturgis.

Everyone who saw it asked about the paint. That job has been wowing people ever since, even gracing the cover of

2

3

Start your parts in black base coat and let them dry overnight. **See fig. 3.** Wet sand them with 600 grit, then respray them with two more coats of black. Why spray black base coat twice? I like to get good coverage on the parts, but I don't want tons of layers sprayed on at one time, or Marblizer settling in the sandscratches. I use plastic wrap to manipulate the House of Kolor Marblizer. Here I used silver, but HOK makes a few different colors, any of which can be used. Tear off a sheet of plastic wrap and have it close by. Apply the first layer of Marblizer. Do one side of a part at a time—first the top of the tank, then the side of the tank, and so on. Spray a medium wet coat of Marblizer.

4

Quickly grab the plastic wrap, stick it against the Marblizer, and move it around. **See fig. 4.** I don't keep the plastic sheet flat. If I'm marblizing the top of a tank and want a long pattern on it, I'll have long folds or wrinkles in the plastic and lay it on like that, then move it. The folds create long, dark

American Iron magazine in 2004. The bike was the talk of the 2003 NACE Show, and one guy even got really angry when I wouldn't tell him how I did it. The problem was (and all the folks who use baseclear clear for everything but final clear may laugh at me now) that the candy urethane coats were not bonding to the Marblizer. I had laid on a few coats of Intercoat Clear, but for fear of blurring the Marblizer I had not applied them heavy enough to bond everything together. However, on the sample fender, I had blasted that Intercoat on.

The lesson here? Sometimes you win, sometimes you lose, and sometimes you beat the odds, but it can be a horror show until you do. And those are times you remember best. So here's the step-by-step for my famous marblizing technique. Maybe some other painters have done this, maybe not, but this is how I do it. If it doesn't work for you and peels or bubbles, just keep trying—but try it first on a test part. Remember, this is not the "approved" way to apply Marblizer. This is the bad girl doing evil things with paint.

5

streaks in the Marblizer surface. Go over all the parts, bit by bit. Keep the gun pressure low. Use a small spray gun, like a Sata Mini Jet. If you desire a dark texture with lots of black showing through and vivid contrast between the black and Marblizer, be careful when spraying the Marblizer. The silver overspray can mute the awesome pattern on the top of the tank as you spray the side of the tank.

For a dark, dramatic effect, don't over-Marblize. **See fig. 5.** If you end up with too much Marblizer and want to see more black or create more black swirls or texture, get some House of Kolor Neutral Marblizer MB-00. Spray a wet layer of that on right where you want to make the

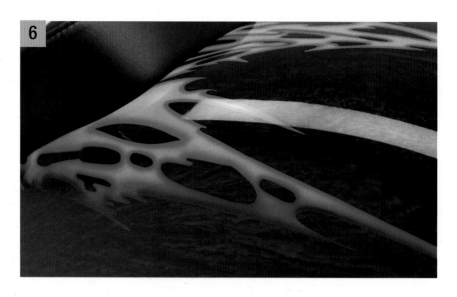

One layer of Marblizer, layered with HOK Purple UK-10. Aaron Stevenson

change, slap a clean piece of plastic wrap on and move it into the pattern you want. Remove the plastic and let the part dry.

This is where you stop if minimal marblizing and lots of black are wanted. Wait 30 minutes and apply a coat of HOK Intercoat Clear. This is critical! If this step is not done, delamination problems may occur. If using urethane top coats, wait 30 minutes before clearing. No wait is needed if you're using base coat clear.

Now, there are two ways the metal or foil effect (seen at the beginning of this chapter) can be done. One is to continue spraying on coats of Marblizer and manipulating them with the plastic. The other is more risky, because the layers won't bond. That's what happened to me in 2002.

The first process is easier, but not as effective. Continue spraying on layers using the method I've just described. Wait 15 to 20 minutes between coats. Go from part to part, using the Neutral Marblizer to redo areas that don't have enough black streaks showing or where the paint looks too even. Let the layers dry 30 minutes. Then apply two medium coats of House of Kolor SG-100

Note the long, dark streaks.

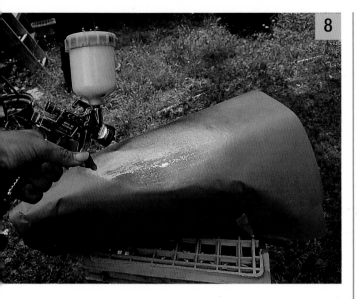

8

10

11

Intercoat Clear. This is the trick: If the Intercoat Clear is sprayed on correctly, it will reach down through the layers of Marblizer and bond them together. If sprayed too dry, it won't penetrate properly. If sprayed too heavy, the Marblizer will soften too much and the dramatic effect will dissipate. Wait 30 minutes then apply three coats of urethane clear or go straight to candy coats, using candy urethane or uro (urethane), base coat or Intercoat Clear mixed with candy concentrate.

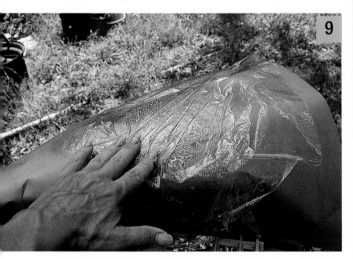

9

12

The second process is the risky one, but the one that achieves that total foil effect seen in **fig. 7**. Please try this first on a test part. Make sure the process works for you and doesn't lift or bubble. It may take a day or two for the bubbles to pop up, and the bubbles won't appear until after the urethane is applied. Even if only base coat clear is used, the bubbles may still be present. Test this process very thoroughly.

Here's how to do it. Wrap high-quality or glossy masking paper around a spare part, like a fat fender or gas tank. Do

the first layer of Marblizing on your parts. Now, work on one part at a time. I use the same piece of plastic for each part, and change the plastic when I move to the next part. Start by spraying a layer of Marblizer on the masking paper. **See fig. 8.**

Slap the plastic wrap on the sprayed masking paper and "pick up" the Marblizer on the plastic. **See fig. 9.**

Quickly lay the plastic over the area being Marblized and move it around. **See fig. 10.** Repeat the process over and over

until the desired effect is achieved. You must work fast, keeping the Marblizer wet as it is transferred. It's easier to see how the process works after you've made the first transfer.

Play around with the wrinkles in the plastic while picking up Marblizer. **See fig. 11.** Here I want long streaks.

Then apply it, wrinkled, on the fender. **See fig. 12.**

Watch for dry bits of Marblizer getting trapped under layers. **See fig. 13.** Check each part after layering on the material. Brush off raised, dry bits with your fingers. As to

The finished product.

Here's the same sample next to a test tank that had even more layers of Marblizer applied.

Two samples of marblizing with liquid graphics. The left fender only has one layer of Marblizer and is cleared with HOK Purple UK-10. The right fender is the sample part I was talking about previously. Four layers of Marblizer and cleared with HOK Tangerine UK-08.

the number of layers to be applied in this way, I've done about four layers like this.

Properly clearing over these layers with the Intercoat Clear is critical to this process. **See fig. 14.** Wait 30 minutes before applying clear. In order for the layers to bond, the Intercoat must penetrate right down to the black. That was the mistake I made in my story—with the sample, I had flooded on the Intercoat Clear that was nearly heavy enough to mottle the Marblizer. I was more careful when working on the actual parts, and that caused my problems.

After all the layers are done, and the Intercoat is on, apply the desired candy or clear coats. **See fig. 15.** Here I used HOK KK-01 Kandy Brandywine Koncentrate mixed with HOK Intercoat Clear. Be sure to wait 30 minutes if using urethane. And that's how I do it—but I can't guarantee this will work perfectly for all painters. (And I don't want that guy to punch me out at the next NACE Show, so I had to include it in this book!) As always, while using any House of Kolor product, make sure you have their tech manual for all their products close by. I can't remember everything, so I find myself opening up that book more often than I want to admit. Refer to this book's Chapter 15 for clearing info.

If a few small isolated bubbles do come up, they can be dug out with a stencil knife, filled, and re-Marblized. If more than just a few raise up, sandblast or peel, but don't say I didn't warn you. But do try again—on a test part. This marblizing technique is an awesome effect that can be successfully painted.

Silver leaf pinstripe flames work great over the Marblizer and under the candy. Note the way the color changes from light to dark throughout the bike.

Three layers of Marblizer with HOK Kandy Violette UK-17 over it.

Three layers of Marblizer with HOK Kandy Apple Red UK-10. Gold metal effect lettering goes great with the red.

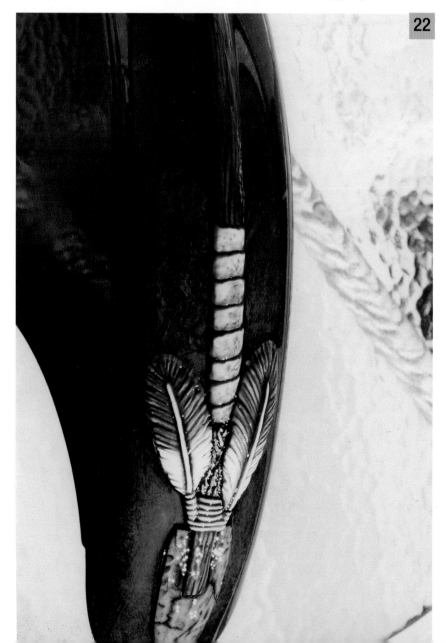

Two layers of Marblizer with HOK Kandy Teal UK-14.

CHAPTER 5
AIRBRUSH ARTWORK, EQUIPMENT, DESIGNS, AND TECHNIQUES

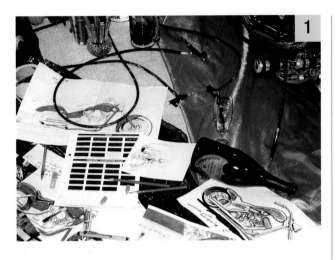

Studio after a rough weekend of airbrushing.

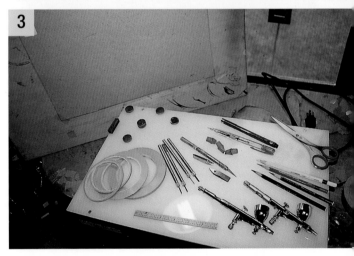

These equipment recommendations and tons of essential handy hints will make any artwork or airbrush process easier.

THE ESSENTIAL EQUIPMENT

Years ago, I knew the location, quality of copies, and business hours of every copy machine within a 30-minute drive from my home. I'd break the speed of sound trying to get to one with great enlargement and reduction capabilities before they closed. There were times when it felt like my life depended on it. Copy machines saved me hours of resizing drawings by hand. They took all guesswork out of it. Then someone invented personal computers, along with scanners and printers, and suddenly instead of stressing at the wheel, I could stay at home and get a whole lot more—and better—work done. If you don't have a computer, most drug stores and many other places have copiers that will reduce and enlarge drawings or photos, but consider the value of your time carefully before you decide you can do without. You'll also find yourself in need of those hard-to-find items you'll only get online through a computer! These days computer equipment is a bargain. A desktop computer paired with a scanner and printer can be bought for less than $700.

A light box is also an essential piece of my equipment. **See fig. 2.** You can buy one online for as little as $55. You can also make one using a plastic crate, a sheet of clear Plexiglas, and a light-bulb fixture. Or just tape whatever you're tracing to a window (during the day, of course) and trace away.

Other things I cannot live without if I am airbrushing are, as seen in the above photo, a drawing board, magnets, pink erasers, a mechanical pencil, a fine line permanent marker, high-quality scissors, Stabilo pencils, Iwata airbrushes, an

X-acto No. 11 knife, Uncle Bill's Sliver Grippers, X-acto No. 4 stencil knives, 3M green Fine Line Tape, and my television. (Sliver Grippers are fine tweezers that are available online for $6.85 at www.magellans.com. Just type in "Sliver Grippers" on Magellans' search feature.)

I keep the drawing board close by for tracing the reverse sides of drawings or to draw stuff by hand. I also tape a piece of thin cardboard on one side of the drawing board, and cut all my stencils on that. Stencils seem to cut better when against a soft surface rather than a hard one. Plus, after all the cuts mar the cardboard surface, I just remove it and tape a new one on. This saves the wooden drawing board surface and makes for quick and easy stencil cutting. I sometimes use a cutting plotter, but I find for most of my applications it's just quicker and easier to cut out my stencils by hand. Besides, they only gave me so many pages for this book and I'd have to add a bunch of pages to cover cutting plotter info.

The magnets hold paper stencils in place on metal parts. Pink erasers, like the pointed ones that go on the end of a pencil, come in very handy—not just for erasing pencil lines and rubbing off frisket adhesive from painted surfaces, but also to erase overspray that creeps in between pieces of tape. I once had just finished touching up a logo on a tank and some overspray had snuck between bits of masking tape. Under the rework, there was plenty of clear, so the overspray rubbed right off with an eraser without affecting the original artwork. Mechanical pencils are great for getting the very fine lines needed on stencils. Fine line permanent markers are used directly in artwork to get superfine detail. Stabilo pencils are great when working on fine details like faces—you can clear coat over them. I know artists who have done entire murals using only Stabilos.

I use the tweezers to grab frisket when removing it and to handle tiny tape ends. It's easier than trying to maneuver and place them with my fingers. I prefer the small No. 4 knives to any others when cutting frisket paper, and they are small enough to maneuver around curves. But No. 11 knives work better for cutting paper stencils. I use a smooth white cutting stone to keep the blades sharp.

I also keep a soft measuring tape handy for referencing around tanks and fenders, as well as 6- and 15-inch steel rulers. Some painters will only use blue fine line tape, as they feels it hugs the curves better than the green, but I prefer the green fine line. I feel it lays down a straighter line than the blue because it is stiffer. It comes in many different widths, and the 1/16-inch tape holds a sharp curve if pressed firmly down. When taped around a sharp curve, it stays down just fine, especially if masking tape is run alongside the unpainted side of the curve. You may need to go back and burnish down the curves just before you spray.

As for the TV, airbrushing can be stressful and tedious. I find having a TV on gives background noise and takes the edge off the atmosphere. Also, it can add to the mood. For instance, if I'm working on a medieval-themed mural, I'll put a barbarian movie on. The right background can help your frame of mind, or draw you even deeper into the job—into another world, even. Some people prefer music. The point is to make your painting atmosphere as pleasant, relaxing, or appropriate as possible.

For stencils I prefer Grafix brand frisket paper, Avery Yellow Paint Mask No. A1830-S (www.averygraphics.com), and MetalFlake Company's Spray Mask (1-800-227-2683). Many airbrush artists successfully use transfer tape as stencil material, but I like to be able to see the background artwork through the mask.

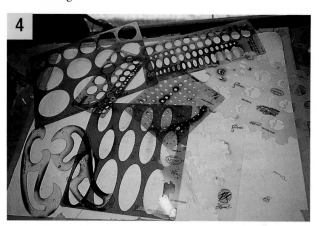

Flexible drafting templates, like circles, ellipses, and ovals, and specialized airbrushing stencils (like Craig Fraser's line of skull stencils) are also things I use quite a bit. **See fig. 4.** You can find these stencils at most online art stores.

FINDING MATERIALS AND EQUIPMENT

Most paint, sandpaper, and taping materials can be found at automotive paint supply stores. Transfer tape and Avery Yellow Paint Mask are found at sign supply stores. Different stores carry different lines of paint, like PPG, Dupont, etc. But most stores carry House of Kolor, which can also be found at online paint stores. Call the store first to find out if it carries the line or brand of paint you want. Artists tools and materials can be found at art supply stores, but I buy most of my stuff online: dixieart.com; bearair.com; dickblick.com; and misterart.com are some of the places at which you can find everything from airbrushes to Stabilo pencils. If you have difficulty finding a product, just go online and use a search Website.

SETTING UP YOUR WORKSPACE

Another thing to keep in mind is that you'll be spending many hours at your airbrush bench, so make it as comfortable as possible. I've been using the same bench for 25 years. It's the prefect height for me. If your workbench is too low, attach a few 2x4 pieces under the legs. You'll want to sit up as straight as possible. Don't let your back hunch or slump, because you'll be in serious pain within a few hours or the next day.

I use boxes and bits of wood to raise my work if I find myself bending over the bench. **See fig. 5.** I have two taped-off boxes that I use to raise tanks and fenders. There is also a gallon can filled with water that I can lean parts against. I sit in a swivel chair so I can rock back. My bench has a foot rest, but much of time I sit cross-legged in my chair. Experiment around with bench and seating positions. Find a way to make it as comfy as possible. Keep a supply of various sized pieces of wood and a few firm boxes handy. That way, you can just grab them and quickly readjust your working height.

You do whatever it takes to be comfortable. In the photo here, I needed the top middle of the tank to be lower. **See fig. 6.** I propped up the front of the tank on a business card box, moved the tank down so the end hung off the bench, and secured the tank in place by taping both sides to the bench.

Sometimes I find that it is easier to airbrush in a certain direction. I airbrush better horizontally (back and forth) than I do vertically (up and down). So I position parts in user friendly directions, like the fender above. **See fig. 7.** This way, I'm pulling a smooth, straight line with the airbrush as I'm shading in taped-off edges or airbrushing a mural.

My airbrush area. There is a system, really, there is.

Keep everything handy and within easy reach. Paint bottles can get out of control. Try to not have more colors mixed up than are being used on that particular job. But always have white, black, and other colors you often use mixed up and ready to spray. After a job is finished, try to go through the work area and put everything paper related to that job in a file. Then clean up the area. You can waste hours trying to find stuff. Take the time to have a system. It's great to be working on an eagle and be able to quickly pull up an older drawing for reference or leftover feather stencils to help with the new eagle mural. Each paint job I do gets a file.

LIGHTING

I use two clamp-on lights, one to the left of me and one to the right, both pointing at my work. One has a spiral fluorescent natural-light bulb in it. The other has a 100-watt incandescent bulb. The overhead light in the room also has a spiral natural-light bulb in it. Between the three lights providing two different kinds of light, I can really see the whole surface I am working on because there are no shadows.

AIRBRUSHES

Most artists have a favorite kind of airbrush. I used Badger 150 siphon feed or bottle feed airbrushes for years. I got great results with them. The range of needles and tips allowed me to go fine hairline to wide spray, and the price was right. Then in the mid 1990s, I switched over to grav-

ity or top feed airbrushes for greater control of fine detail. I now use Iwata HP-C and Micron C airbrushes for most of my detail work. I have six airbrushes set up. I also use a Satagraph 2 top feed. With both brands of airbrush, I like the way I can remove the spray regulators and get a very fine line for details. I can also put them back on and use the brushes for shading and fades. For larger spray needs, I use a Sata Dekor 2000 artbrush, Iwata Eclipse bottle feeds, and an old Badger 150 with a large needle and tip. The Sata artbrush has a wide range of nozzle sizes from 0.2 to 1.0 millimeters. For beginning airbrushers, I recommend going to an art supply store and checking out the under-$100 airbrushes. Find one that feels comfortable in your hand. Look for one with a smooth trigger action. Iwata Eclipse and Badger 150 are two good choices for beginners.

I use a homemade air manifold made out of pipe fittings. **See fig. 9.** Commercial manifolds on the market tend to be pricey, and a little common sense goes a long way. At some discount stores, you can find aluminum blocks with quick disconnect fittings already installed. Go to most quality auto parts or hardware stores and go through their air hose or pipe fitting trays. Take along the fittings for your airbrush hoses and design your own set up.

AIRBRUSH MAINTENANCE

All kinds of things can go wrong with airbrushes. Dried, clogged paint is the biggest problem. Know your airbrush. Learn how to take it apart and thoroughly clean it with lacquer thinner. I remove the needle and use good quality cotton swabs to clean out the color cup on my gravity-feed airbrushes. I do this at end of each workday. Little round bristle brushes can also be used to clean out passages. See Chapter 16 for more detail.

PAINT FOR AIRBRUSHING

Lacquer atomizes down finer than any other kind of automotive paint—some airbrushers refuse to use any other paint. I switched over to uncatalyzed base coat enamels 10 years ago, and it took some getting used to. As for brands to recommend, I can't because there is no one brand of paint that is the best. As of right now, the brand of paint I use is House of Kolor. I have had very good results with it and is has proved to be very, very durable, dependable, and easy to work with when used properly. Then there is (what many say) the "future" of paint, which is water-based paint. Water base has come a long, long way. Many airbrush artists love the new Auto Air line of water-based paint. More and more painters are using it, and their range of colors is quite extensive and getting more extreme everyday. Though I don't have enough experience to talk much about it, like any paint, the more you use it, the better you'll be at using it. Like it or not, water base is the future, and the sooner a painter starts using it, the more experience is gained and the better that product will work. By the time this book goes to press, I'll have been playing around quite a bit with water base. Some of the colors are very exciting, but like any paint, I need to get used to it before I use it on customers' jobs. Other companies are also developing waterbased paint, so these products will only keep improving.

Every kind and brand of paint has its own qualities and the airbrusher needs to become familiar with them. Some painters like brand X and some swear by brand Y. The best thing to do is to try out a kind of paint by buying a pint of black, a pint of white, and some reducer. Spend some time and play around with it. Get used to it. Is it too grainy, or does it make the airbrush spit no matter how much it is reduced? Try another brand. I have seen all kinds of awesome mural work and asked what brand of paint the artist used. I get a different answer each time.

Keeping an inventory of pearls and specialty colors for graphics and flames comes in very handy. Pearl base coats dry quickly and cover great with minimal coats. I keep an inventory of basic color pearls, such as blue, teal, and purple, and find I keep using them. Some painters have their own mixing systems and can mix up pearls of the specific paint brand they use. For the painter who doesn't have a mixing system, keeping a small inventory of House of Kolor pearls will come in extremely handy. PPG is also coming out with more specialty paints, and I look forward to having some fun with those. More paint companies with custom paint lines means more choices for the custom painter, which is a good thing.

I keep my airbrush paint mixtures in airbrush bottles with caps on them. I agitate them often while working, stirring them with a screwdriver.

SAFETY

The essential component at the airbrush bench is proper ventilation.

I have always set up my bench in front of a window with a fan in it. My current shop has a variable-speed, 8 1/2-inch round fan bolted into a Plexiglas window. I also have a small fan off to the side, behind me, pushing fresh air past my face. If I'm doing anything other than very light detail work, I wear a respirator. In addition to the window fan's benefit of getting that paint-fume air out of my studio as quickly as possible, during the day, I love the natural light that comes in the window. A northern-exposure window is the optimum choice, but an eastern exposure will do. You don't want to work with the sun hitting you in the face. I've had work areas that were in shops, surrounded by concrete and equipment with no windows. It definitely had a negative effect on my work. My best work was done sitting in front of a window that looked out into a world of trees and nature. Folks ask me how I can do such tedious work for hours on end. The answer is simple. Over the years I've learned what works for me and what gets me the best results in my artwork: Calm, quiet, peaceful sur-

roundings with no distractions work for me. Some artists thrive in shops that give them contact with people, while others prefer extreme privacy. It doesn't matter. Find what works for you, the kind of atmosphere you feel happy and relaxed in, and set up shop.

Other safety considerations with airbrushing are paint storage, ventilation, and cleanup. I keep very little paint in my studio—only the colors for the artwork I am doing that day. All other paint is stored in a climate-controlled shed that is not attached to my home or shop. More paint cans sitting around the studio mean more fumes, which can spell trouble. For example, a buddy of mine was painting urethane clear coat one hot night, wearing only a pair of cotton shorts. With no real ventilation in his shop, the place was full of fumes and urethane was drifting around. Of course, his exposed skin was covered with sticky urethane. He sat down with a rag and lacquer thinner and proceeded to wipe his body off. About that time I came out to see how things were going. He was sitting there on the steps, bleary eyed, and told me he didn't feel very well. He'd just soaked poison into his skin, and now it was flowing throughout his body, making him sick. Now when I clean my guns or airbrushes I always wear vinyl gloves. If I can possibly help it, lacquer thinner never touches my hands. And always use common sense. If you're breathing fumes, your thinking will get fuzzy and common sense will go out the window.

REFERENCE LIBRARY AND IDEAS

Build a good photo reference library. A $25 investment in a book on eagles is money well spent, since that book will give you ideas and great photos to work from for years. This is 25 years of collecting reference books. **See fig. 10.** I can find a photo of nearly anything I need to airbrush. And what's not there is most likely on my computer— another reason to invest in one. I have many photos of artwork I like loaded on my computer. To get ideas, I sift through a lot of this stuff, or sometimes, an idea just pops into my head. Then I find the photos that help me develop that idea. Other times I have to go through my reference material to get ideas. Maybe I'll see a graphic that I like only parts of. I'll use that, and then change it around. Save as many photos and ideas as possible, but make sure to have a system in place to organize them all. I even have a box filled with old photos, filed in envelopes, with headings such as wolves, women, and backgrounds.

FABRICATION PHOTOS

When you're dealing with custom bikes, get fabrication photos of the sheet metal parts assembled on the frame. That way you'll see how the parts sit on the bike. Knowing the angle of the tank can help in lining up the graphics beforehand. Things like seeing how and where the rear fender mount crosses over the rear fender is essential when figuring out the artwork design.

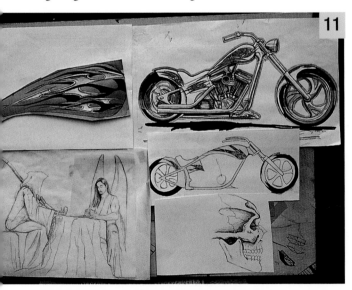

PREPAINT DRAWINGS

I sometimes make drawings before I do artwork. **See fig. 11.** This way I see, plan, and fine-tune my work before I even touch the sheet metal. I use a combination of my reference library, a computer, a light box, and hand drawing to arrange and think out the drawings. This is where fabrication photos are essential if working on a custom bike. A simple trick: Take the photo of the fabricated bike, or whatever

bike is being painted, and make an enlarged copy of it. Then with whiteout, paint out the stuff that will be painted— tanks, fenders, maybe frame and oil tank. Now make a few copies of that. Or place an enlarged copy of the picture on a light box or tape it to a window. Put tracing paper over it and trace the outlines of the bike and its parts. Make a few copies of that. Now you will have plenty of "blanks" of the bike design to play around with. The finished drawings can be submitted to the customer who can approve or advise you in making changes.

In addition to base coat samples, many times I also test my artwork colors and technique. Countless hours can be saved with simple testing. The customer can also approve the test part, and the painter's sanity can be saved, because the customer can't later claim he's dissatisfied with the design and/or colors.

MAKING SIDES MATCH

This can apply to sides of a tank, or whenever a design needs to be repeated or reversed. Once the design is laid out and taped off or cut out on one side of the part, tape a piece of tracing paper over it. (Refer to Chapters 8, 9, and 13 for detailed photos.) Using a pencil, trace along the edges of the design. If the design will be repeated, flip it over and place the tracing paper on a light table or window. Trace the design with pencil, flip it over, place it on the surface to be painted, and trace along the lines. Now if you want to reverse the design for the opposite side of tank or fender, simply flip it over. Presto! The pencil lines are already there.

13

15

Take measurements from the first side to get reference points to aid in lining up the design. **See fig. 13.** For tank measurements, I use the seam down the center of the tank and a point on the front of the tank. In the picture above, I used the tunnel on the front of the gas tank, measured from the ends of the design to the edge of the tunnel, and then marked those places on the other side.

14

them with a pink eraser. Once the artwork is painted and the tape or spray mask removed, check for smudges and pencil lines that wander from under the artwork, and erase or damp sand them.

Here I needed flames to be identical on both sides. **See fig. 16.**

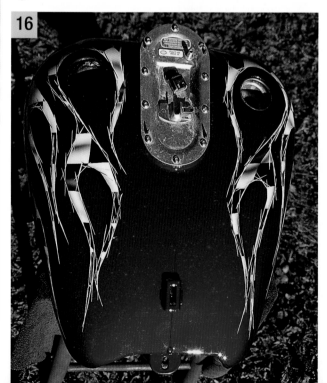

16

Line up the tracing on the other side and trace along the lines. **See fig. 14.** It will leave an imprint of the design on the surface.

I use fine line tape to double-check points of the design before I cut it out or tape it off. **See fig. 15.** After the design is taped off, check for pencil lines on the surface and erase

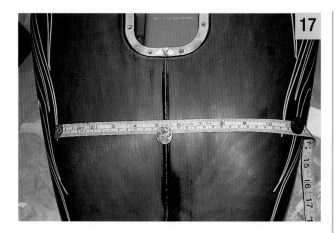

17

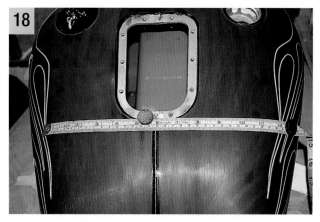

18

On a different flamed tank here, you can see where I used a measuring tape in two places to reference from the seam on top of the tank to the flame ends. **See figs. 17 and 18.**

Here are two fenders in which I had to run the design on both halves of the fender, splitting the fenders down the middle. **See fig. 19 and 20.** Before laying out the design, I ran fine line tape down the middle of the fenders, laid out the design on one side, and transferred the design to tracing paper. I flipped it over, lined up the centerlines, and traced along the design lines, leaving a pencil drawing of the design on the surface. (Notice those green pinstripes. The customer did not want lime green. But as you can see, it truly complements the blue and purple. Choosing stripe colors can be easy or difficult and can make all the difference in the success of a paint job. Sometimes I find that contrasting colors work best. But some base colors are more effective with stripes that are of a similar tone.)

ARTWORK MATCHING AND REVERSING—ANOTHER TRICK

Another modern trick to get sides to match is to first do the artwork on one side of the tank. Then once it's done, take a digital picture of it. Load the photo into your computer, reverse it with a graphics program, and print it out. For murals, resize it so it's the same size as the actual artwork. Tape it to the tank near the mural or have it close by. This computer trick can make doing reversed artwork a whole lot easier. Paper stencils can also be made from any copies of the reversed photo.

REWORKING ARTWORK

I tend to do my rework after the first coats of clear are applied. If my first artwork attempt isn't perfect, I don't sweat it. I save my artwork under clear coat. Then I look it

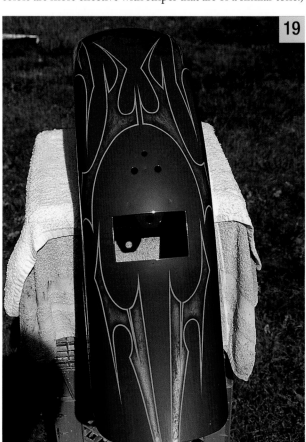

19

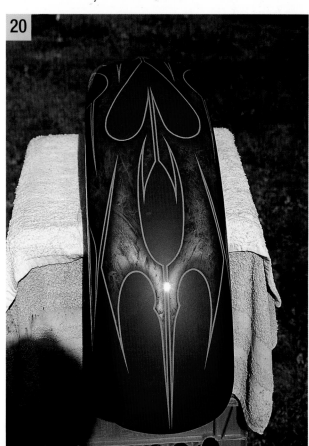

20

over, checking where I need to make changes. Many times, I'll use a clipboard with either a digital photo or stick figure drawing of the parts and mark on the photo or drawing where I need to do rework. This is especially helpful when touching up graphics and flames—there's a lot to remember, and all those little lines aren't always perfect on the first try. Don't freak over artwork mistakes. Most of the time they can be fixed with rework. Even the very best painters have to go back and fix stuff.

MISCELLANEOUS DESIGN LAYOUT HINTS

Let's say you need to move a stencil or cutout. You have it all taped on, but it needs to be moved 1/4 inch to the left. Lay out fine line tape all around the stencil, except on the side in the direction it needs to be moved. Now, lay a line of tape 1/4 inch from the edge of the stencil. Now the stencil can be peeled up and put exactly where it needs to go because you've set a location reference.

Another hint: After I draw out designs on spray mask or the surface of the part, I lay fine line tape along the lines and trace with a pen or pencil to help smooth out the lines.

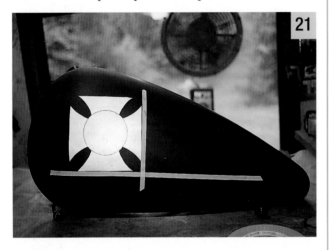

Here's another one. Let's say you need to line up a design based on the level at which the parts sit when on the bike. Position the part, maybe using blocks of wood, then lay out a straight line indicating the level. Now, just line up the cutout of the stencil along that line. **See fig. 21.** Also, look at the angle of lines of the part itself. Some graphic situations require the design to sit in the middle of the part, so run the reference line down that center. Consider both of these factors when lining up and laying out designs. Sometimes I can do it by eye, but I always make a few quickie measurements to help me center the line. If the stencil is for lettering, run the line along where you want the lettering to be. Now you know the lettering will be straight, and not crooked, once the tank is on the bike.

When sketching out designs on curved surfaces like fenders, wrap it in tracing paper, but cut slots in the paper so the paper will fold neatly around the curves. **See fig. 22.**

Here's what the tracing paper design looked like for Chapter 9 Liquid Graphics. **See fig. 23.**

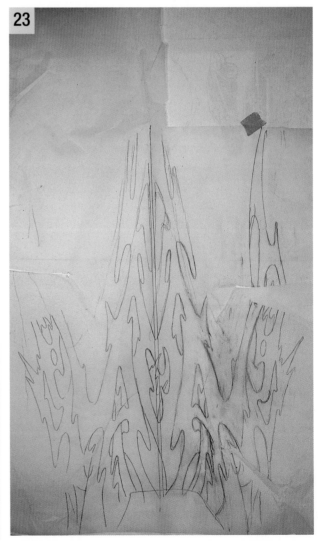

Here is the finished product.

MIXED BAG OF TRICKS

Do the less noticeable parts first! For example, the right side of the tank is the most noticed part of the sheet metal. Do that side last. Many times, as the artwork process progresses, I find that my technique gets sharper the more I get used to it. It's not pleasant to find the highest degree of artwork on a portion of the bike other than the most noticeable parts—mainly the right side of the tank and the front fender. Do those sections last.

Know your peak times of working ability. Know when in the day you're at your sharpest. I used to put in 18-hour days, and found (not surprisingly) that I made the most mistakes toward the end of that shift. Save nonpeak hours for maintenance, cleaning airbrushes and bottles, filing duties, etc.

Don't ever assume you automatically know the direction the parts go on the bike, their physical orientation—see this dash? **See fig. 25.** See the problem? It's upside down. I did this many, many years ago. I decided to buy another dash and keep the wolf mural for reference and to remind me to always double-check the parts and know how they fit.

Take care when wiping down finished artwork with precleaner! Beware of using precleaner on uncleared artwork. The cleaner can penetrate and soften the paint, and you'll be removing artwork. I've actually seen marks from wiping with precleaner causing artwork residue to "wipe" across base coat. I never use precleaner on any uncleared artwork. Since I use such thinned-down paint mixtures, I seldom use base coat clear to seal my artwork. It tends to wash out, mottle, or dull the artwork. I'll carefully wipe precleaner around the artwork, removing any frisket adhesive. Some painters use a mix of precleaner and water. Some companies, like HOK, make a product (KC-20) designed for just that purpose.

When papering off completed portions of artwork to protect them from dripping airbrushes, I always cover the paper with masking tape. It forms a better barrier, so paint won't bleed through. I don't like to stick much tape to the artwork, as problems can arise from doing so.

Try not keep parts, other than those you're working on, in the work area of your shop or studio. If possible, have a separate storage area for them, like a shed or spare bedroom. If that is not possible, keep the parts well covered. The chances of getting overspray on them are very good, even if you have an awesome ventilation system.

Also, overspray has a habit of finding its way onto the part you're working on. If I'm working on a tank and have one side finished, I take a digital picture, and then paper off that side to protect it. I'll load the picture into my computer and reverse it with any graphics program. Even MSPaint will work. Now it can be printed out and used as a reference for the reverse side of the tank. No camera? Keep the bottom of the paper loose, so you can turn the tank, lift the paper and peek under it.

Also remember that if you are airbrushing in your home, oil from cooking may be in the air and can land on the surface of the parts, causing contamination that may have an effect on the paint. Keep the studio door shut when cooking, and cover those parts.

Always pull tape back against itself to break the paint edge. **See fig. 26.** Don't wait too long to remove tape. The number of coats of paint you applied will determine how long to wait before the tape can be pulled up. Not waiting long enough can result in the tape lifting the paint, because the layers are too fresh. Wait too long, and the paint will chip and splinter. Wait 15 minutes and check to see if the paint edge breaks away cleanly. It's different in each painting situation. You just have to keep an eye on it and keep checking to see if the paint is at optimum tape removal time. If the paint edge is very thick and a "bridge" has formed between the tape and paint surface, use extreme care: Cut along the tape line with a very sharp No. 11 stencil knife. Tweezers will help to lift away the cut paint. Then pull up the tape. If the paint had dried too much, use a razor blade or stencil knife and carefully slice along the tape edge. Then use the tweezers to lift away the paint crust.

When painting shadows under flames, graphics, or anything, think of how the light hits the graphic to achieve that three-dimensional effect. For example, on the side of a tank, the light source will be coming from above the tank, so the shadow will be under the flame. On the top of a fender, the light is also coming from above, but it is centered, so the right side of the fender top will have the shadow over to the right of the flame. On the left half, the shadow will be over to the left of the flame.

With gravity-feed airbrushes, it is easy to spill paint. If paint drips onto an already-cleared surface, let it dry, then damp sand it off with 800 grit. Don't use solvent. If paint drips on freshly laid artwork, let it dry, then airbrush over it and rework that area. If it has dripped on a flame, then run over onto the cleared base coat, respray that part of the flame, then damp sand the drip off the base coat. This is why I love having urethane clear over my base coats or finished artwork—lots of room for boo-boos. Many times, the outline of the drip will still be visible, but after a round of clear coat and little more retouching, it will disappear.

I keep two mixtures of each color I am using at that time, a thicker one for darker shading, and a thinner mix for less grainy, lighter shading. Sometimes I even have three mixes when I'm using black and white.

If dealing with a very thick paint edge, use a razor blade to trim it down, but this only works properly if a pinstripe will be applied. Sometimes a paint edge is so thick that the weight of clear coats will fold it over and trap air underneath. I always trim thick paint edges down. I hold the razor at a shallow angle, not letting the razor touch anything other than the top of the paint edge, and slowly and carefully shave it down. If there is a raggy loose edge, I remove the excess material by either trimming it with a stencil knife or sticking masking tape against it, then pulling it up. The paint crust will come up with the tape. If more than just the loose bits of paint come up with the tape, it's bad and good at the same time: bad because you've got to rework those areas and good because this problem area would have come back later to haunt you due to lack of adhesion.

To remove bits of the adhesive residue that comes from leaving masking tape on way too long, use precleaner.

There is no limit to what can be used as a tool. Here I used netting from an onion bag to airbrush gator skin. **See fig. 27.**

If using base coat for airbrushing, the reduced paint will break down after a while. So if the airbrush spray is getting grainy, mix up a new batch.

To aid in getting that photorealistic look, try to work from photos of the subject being airbrushed. I even tape photos right next to where I am airbrushing. Put a photo in a plastic bag to protect it.

Always do what I call a "wet-sand-paint-check" after the artwork is done and stencils are removed. You're checking for any contamination that has happened during the artwork process—over-spray, paint that snuck past tape lines, pencil lines, whatever. Very closely, look the part over in the sun. Using 800 grit, very, very carefully wet sand everything that doesn't have artwork on it. If the artwork doesn't have a sharp or distinct edge to it, don't even come close to the border of the fade. For example, if a mural of a sky blends out from the base color, don't sand that blend. Do this in the sun, because the sun will show every little flaw. For pencil or design lines, look very carefully along the edges of flames and graphics, fold the sandpaper over so you have nice neat edge, and if there is an area with artwork, softly sand right up to the edge of that line without touching it.

In-process photo of chief in headdress. The feathers were each taped off and airbrushed individually. Next, a beaded headband will be added. The face will go on last.

Finished chief.

A perfect example of lettering that couldn't be done without a plotter cutting out the stencil. I did not have a plotter when I did this. I gave a copy of the lettering to a sign shop, and they made me the stencil—for $35.

Little ideas can have big impact. A simple card hand, but the skull in the spade gives it a touch of evil.

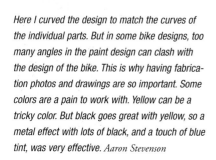

Here I curved the design to match the curves of the individual parts. But in some bike designs, too many angles in the paint design can clash with the design of the bike. This is why having fabrication photos and drawings are so important. Some colors are a pain to work with. Yellow can be a tricky color. But black goes great with yellow, so a metal effect with lots of black, and a touch of blue tint, was very effective. *Aaron Stevenson*

33

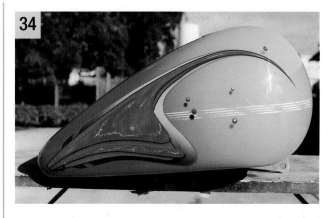

34

Soft shadowing can really bring life to a graphic. Here I used round shapes from a plastic drafting template to shadow the little spheres. Putting the shadow not directly under the sphere, leaving a gap between it and the shadow, gives the three-dimensional illusion.

LEFT: Sometimes less is more. This tank shows that a simple slash down the center works better than a busier design. It complements the shape of the tank and doesn't make it look too fat or too long. Aaron Stevenson

BELOW: Designing a paint job for a set of tanks and fenders usually involves a main mural on each side of the tank and a smaller murals relating to it on the fenders. Here I even painted simple murals of field flowers on the sidecovers. These were done over stock factory paint. (An easy way to get through a job quickly is to do it over the stock paint.) I carefully wet sanded the decal off, taking care not to sand too deeply through the under coats.

35

36

I love painting oil tanks so that both sides perfectly match. Too bad they look best from an angle that can't be seen once the tank is in place on the bike. I run fine line tape down the front center of the tank. Then with tracing paper over the tank, I draw out my design from one side, marking where the centerline is. Then I simply flip the paper over and trace the design on the other side.

37

38

I took parts from a Harley and actually put them on my scanner and made copies of them, enlarging or reducing as needed. With the major parts I made overall vinyl stencils, and made paper stencils for details and smaller parts. Longer, straighter parts were created by using fine line tape and various shapes on drafting templates. Aaron Stevenson

39

Oddly shaped parts can be a challenge to work on. Here I found a balance of graphics and murals to wrap around this airdam.

41

Frisket stencils used for the feathers. The beaded area was taped off with fine line, window screen material was lined up over the area, and the beads were airbrushed. The screen creates borders between the beads.

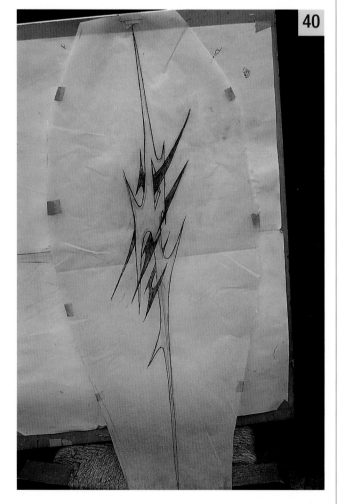

40

Predrawing for airbox cover.

42

Aaron Stevenson

CHAPTER 6
NOT SO BASIC FLAMES

EQUIPMENT AND ARTWORK

I'm not listing paint products since the products that can be used are endless.

- 1/16" 3M green Fine Line Tape
- Masking tape various sizes—1/4", 3/4", and 2"
- Transfer tape—can be bought at sign supply shops
- 600-, 800-, and 1000-grit wet sandpaper
- Metalflake Company's Spray Mask (1-800-227-2683)
- Stabilo pencils (any art store)
- Tracing paper (get the most transparent you can find)
- Iwata HP-C airbrush
- Iwata Micron C airbrush
- Satagraph 2 airbrush
- X-acto No. 4 stencil knife (check online art stores)
- Uncle Bill's Sliver Grippers—available online for $4.95 at www.scoutgear.com. Type "sliver" in search field.
- 00 Mack striping brush
- Newspaper
- Cheapie 2" paint brush
- Scissors
- Razor blade
- Lead pencil

are probably as many ways of doing flames as there are flame designs. So don't listen to the complainers, listen to your customers. Plain and simple: flames are cool.

Taping off the flame is the easy part. The traditional flame technique involves laying down a flame outline using a very thin tape. **See fig. 2.** Some folks use 1/8-inch masking tape or blue fine line tape. Some use 1/16-inch green fine line tape. Everyone says their method is the best, but I think folks just use what works best for them.

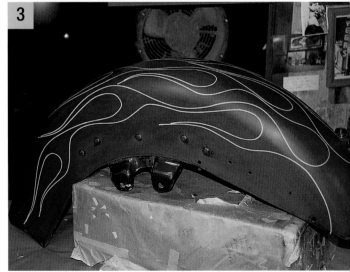

Some people, always on the lookout for something different, complain that too many bikes have flames—that flames are out of style. But flames will never be out of style, because new flame techniques and designs are constantly being invented, and reinvented. And there

I enjoy painting flames and like to have fun with designs. Play around with ideas a little bit before you start laying on paint. Arranging the flame design to best fit the piece is the hard part. **See fig. 3.** Don't just rush through it. It is quite unpleasant to untape a tank or fender after hours of work and layers of paint to see that the design looks awkward or just doesn't complement the line of the sheet metal.

My main goal is flame symmetry: having the flame design nicely balanced, but not too generic, not too uniform, and not too busy. **See fig. 4.**

I use two methods of laying out flames. With one, I lay out the flame with 1/16-inch green fine line tape. I prefer it to the blue tape, because it is stiffer and lays down a smoother flame line. Its advantage over the masking tape is that it leaves a crisp, sharp line—perfect for ghost flames or metal-effect flames that will not be pinstriped. (Most folks who use masking tape pinstripe their flames.) Once the flames are laid out, take a very short break, but not too long a break, as the tape edge on the sharp curves of the flames can tend to lift over time. You might even want to secure the sharp curves by running one-quarter inch masking tape against the fine line tape on the side of the flame that is not

being painted. Go get a cold drink. Then go back and look at your design. Always stand back and study it. It's too easy to miss something obvious if you only look at it close up.

After the flame is laid out, cut out small sheets of transfer tape. **See fig. 5.** Transfer tape is mostly used as a cover sheet for vinyl sign lettering and can be bought at any sign-supply shop. Lay the sheets down piece-by-piece and trim off the flame area with a No. 4 stencil knife.

With the No. 4 knife, cut along the top of the 1/16-inch tape, using only enough pressure to cut through the transfer tape, and not enough to cut into the fine line tape below. Use sliver tweezers to grab the edge of the transfer tape for removal. **See fig. 6.** I also use tweezers to handle fine line tape ends. You may even want to check under the tape to see just how far you're cutting into the surface. If the base color is very hard to touch up and you're worried about having a cut line running along the flame, then simply use regular masking tape to tape off the flame.

Don't hesitate to use masking tape. **See fig. 7.** Try to use methods that save time. Sometimes this involves using materials that cost more money, such as wider, 2-inch masking tape to quickly tape off oddly shaped areas. What good is it to save on materials if it takes longer to do the job? Always check your tape edges after you lay them out, to make sure the tape isn't puckering up or lifting on the edges. I use my fingernails to burnish down any lifting or

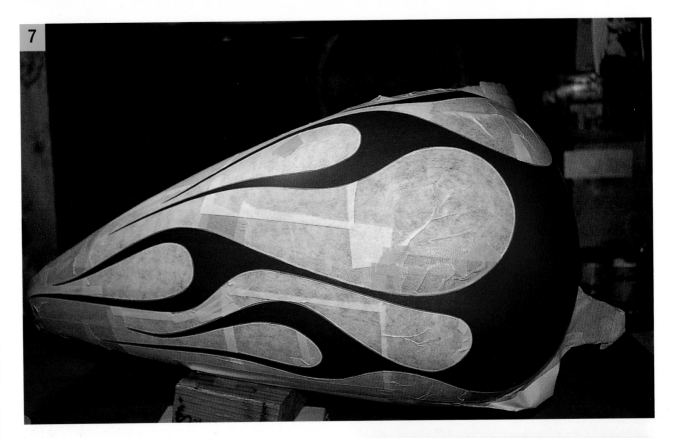

7

8

bubbling tape edges. Another thing to watch for is tiny little spaces that haven't been covered by tape. I take two breaks away from my work while laying out flames. Take a second break after the flame is taped off. When you go back to look at it, you'll find lots of small areas that paint will sneak through. Many tricks shown in the next illustrated step-by-step can be used for painting flames the traditional way and help provide a painless flame job. (To repeat the flame design on the other side of the tank, refer to Chapters 5 and 13 for detailed information and photos.) OK, now spray those flames however you want.

In this example I sprayed them white, let them dry, damp sanded with 600 grit, applied spray mask, drew on checkers, and cut out lines of checkers with a No. 4 stencil knife. I then picked out the black checks with the tweezers and sprayed black—not too heavy so the paint edge wouldn't be overly thick. I next removed the spray mask using the tweezers and lightly airbrushed soft shadows and highlights with a very-reduced black-and-white. To figure shadow placement, just draw slashes on the outer mask and give them a nice slant, then airbrush with soft black. That way, the shadows have a natural wave to them. Add the soft white highlight in between. **See fig. 8.**

The one thing I don't do is freehand pinstriping. There are many awesome books out there on pinstriping. This example here has what folks call "slash" pinstriping and is the only kind of freehand striping I can do. To see a taped-off pinstripe process, check out Chapter 10.

Finished result of fender.

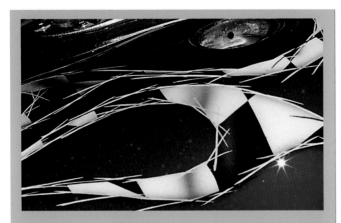

SLASH-STRIPING

I do it using a 00 Mack striping brush. I set up two bottles of contrasting base coat color mixed 1:1, or maybe a little less, with reducer. I dip the brush in the bottle, then drag it along a newspaper to load the brush—that is, evenly distribute the paint throughout the brush hairs. This also takes away any excess paint, the weight of which will drag the brush down. First, I lay a few practice slashes on the newspaper. If I'm happy with those, I try a few on the flames. Now I've already got layers of clear over my flames at this point, so if the slashes are too thick or wavy, I can simply damp sand them off with 800 grit and try again. The clear protects the flame work I've done so far. The secret to good slash striping is to keep a light touch. Just let the tip of the brush touch the surface. If you end up with a few fatties in the mix of stripes, just thinly and lightly stripe your contrasting color through the center of the fat stripes. This will net you three thin stripes from every fat one. And don't expect great results the first time. Practice a bunch, and be patient. Then try out your newfound technique on the real stuff.

Most of the time, flames need to be striped with a flawless, thin, smooth line. I usually take flamed parts to a professional—someone who can freehand stripe as well as I can airbrush. But once in a while, deadlines or designs require I lay out the pinstripe with 1/16-inch fine line tape, then mask it off using 1/16-inch fine line tape (for the most part) and frisket paper trimmed to fit to the inside points of the flames. Check out Chapter 10 for process details and photos. Then I spray it with the airbrush. The flames seen in the next example didn't need to be striped. Ghost flames usually don't need striping, either.

For this next example I used a stock Harley 100th Anniversary paint job as a base after laying on a few coats of clear tinted with candy blue. This brightened up the original color and set it apart from the others. I simply added a few flames that worked with the stock stripe and emblems. Using Norton Soft Touch pads (I love these things), I carefully sanded around the emblems. **See fig. 9.**

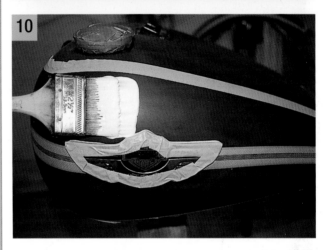

The pads make it possible to sand right up to the edge of the emblem and not scratch it. They come in several grits and quickly take care of oddball sanding duties.

The second method of laying out flames uses Metalflake Company's Spray Mask product, and that's what I'll be demonstrating in the step-by-step. Don't spray it on. Use a thin, soft, cheapie two-inch paint brush and brush on four coats. **See fig. 10.** Don't reduce it. If it is thinned down, its surface structure will be too weak to pull up, and it will break apart as you try to pull. If you use too much Spray Mask, it will be difficult to cut. Four medium-to-heavy layers should do the trick. First, using 3/4-inch masking tape, border off the areas to be covered with spray mask. This way you use less material and give it a firm edge that makes it easier to remove. This sheet metal has emblems, which I also taped off before applying the mask. Leave a very slight gap between the tape and surface, because part of the flame design will run against the emblem. I want the paint to come just up to the emblem but not onto it.

Spray mask goes on milky blue. **See fig. 11.** It dries to a clear, transparent blue. Make sure each mask layer has dried clear before you apply the next one, or it will take forever to dry. If you try to cut out your design before it is completely dry, the wet areas will not cut well or adhere to the surface, and will pull away. I usually let it dry overnight.

The great thing about Spray Mask is that you can use Stabilo pencils to draw out and play around with your flame design. **See fig. 12.** If you don't like the design, simply use a damp cloth to wipe off the marks and try again. Look closely and you can see where I made a few corrections to my design, using a red pencil.

Run 1/8-inch tape along the drawn lines and trace with a pen to get a nice, straight line. **See fig. 13.**

Once you're happy with a flame design, cut it out with a No. 4 knife. I like to place the part at an angle that's comfortable for me and cut along the lines at that angle, pulling

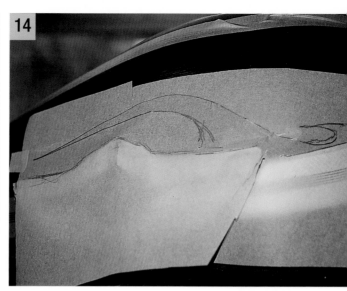

the knife toward me rather than away. You want the line to be smooth and crisp, not choppy. And don't press too hard with the knife. You only want to cut through the spray mask, not into the paint surface. If the knife is not cutting a sharp line, sharpen the blade. I keep a smooth, white sharpening stone around for this. Lay the blade down nearly flat on the surface and wipe it along the stone a few times, sharpening the edge. If that doesn't work, change the blade. Now the paint surface below the mask can get cut, but try to keep that cut as shallow as possible. Using the sliver tweezers, carefully pull out the flame interior—stencil knife in hand—ready to cut away any stringers that are still attached. Tape tracing paper over the designs and trace in order to transfer them to the other side. **See fig. 14.** Mark where the stock pinstripes run, and use them to help line up the paper on the opposite side of the tank.

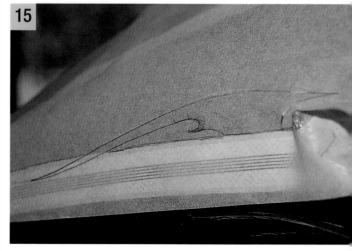

Cut the paper out in places where it comes against the emblems in order to help it lay flat. **See fig. 15.** Remove the tracing paper and line it up on the opposite side of tank.

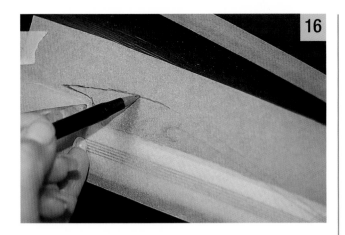

16

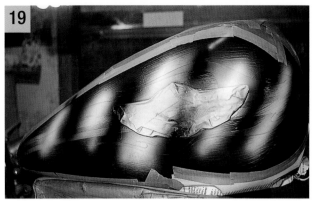

19

Trace the design. Fig. 16. See Chapters 5 and 13 for details on producing reverse designs for the other side of the tank. After taping up any open areas, I'm good to start airbrushing. I'm trying to get a metal effect, that is, I'm trying to make the flames look as if they're cut out of metal. Mix up some *fairly* thinned-down base coat white and black, along with *very* thinned-down base coat white and black. Mix some thinned black with some colored tint (in this case, two kinds of blue—a greenish indigo and a cobalt) that match the tone of the stock paint.

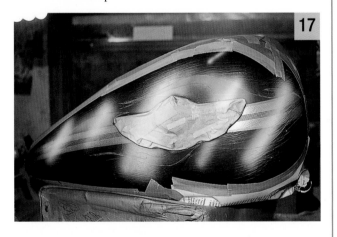

17

Lay down slanted dashes of white, evenly spaced along the flame strip. **See fig. 17.**

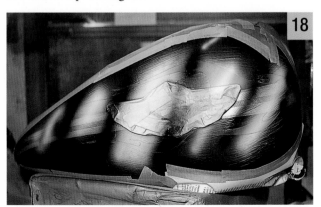

18

In the reverse areas, lay down some black slashes, fading them into the white. **See fig. 18.**

Then with the colored tint, lightly spray over the black, furthering the fade into the white. **See fig. 19.** Now go back with very-thinned white and soften the fade. Also, add a hard line in the direction of the slant, highlighting the white to look like a kind of reflection. If too much white overspray drifted into the dark areas, softly fade in more black and colored tint to richen it.

20

Let it dry a bit, then using the 1/16-inch green fine line tape, tape off a narrow space along the top edge of the flames. **See fig. 20.** Spray this in tones reverse to the flames—black where the white is, and vice-versa. This gives the flames a three-dimensional edge.

Try not to let the paint edge get too thick with your flames. I tend to airbrush my flames, with most of the color concentrated toward the middle of the flame. If I'm doing a faded flame with darker colors airbrushed around the edges, I spray the middle with the lighter colors. This allows the color to fade near the edge, and then I go over the edges with the darker color.

After the flames have dried, but are not so dry that the edge flakes, use the sliver tweezers and remove the spray mask. Always pull any flame-taping material back over itself in the opposite direction, back and away from the way it is laid down. Carefully brush away any loose paint edges and softly wet sand with 800 grit the areas *not* flamed to remove

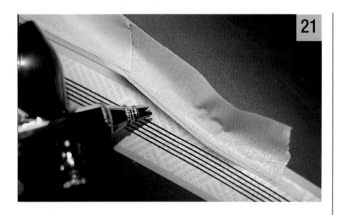

21

any paint that has snuck past the tape and to remove the impressions from the tape that bordered the Spray Mask.

I also added a shadow where the flame overlapped the stock stripe. **See fig. 21.** I simply taped off the flame and the area above the stripe and used a thinned-down black to spray a soft shadow.

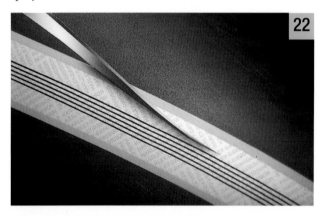

22

Just enough shadow. Not too dark. **See fig. 22.**

23

Retape the emblems, taking care to keep a gap from the paint just big enough to allow for the thickness of the clear coats, or there'll be a paint bridge that you'll have to cut through later. **See fig. 23.** Now it's ready for clear. Go to Chapter 15 for instructions on clear coating and rework. Also while any rework is being done, check the flame tips to see if any stencil cuts extend beyond the tips. If so, tape off those tips, extending them to cover the cut, and touch up with an airbrush, extending the flame.

24

25

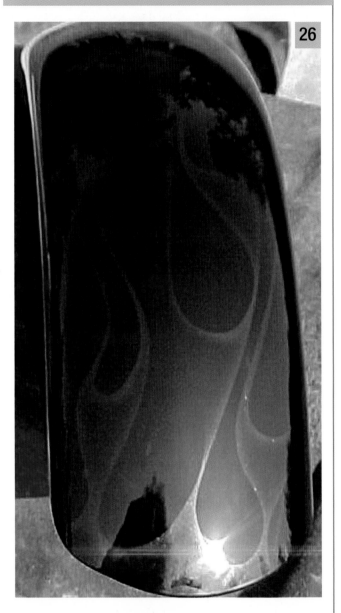

26

GHOST FLAMES

The trick to doing ghost flames is simply spraying as light a line as possible around the edges of the taped-off flame. *Ghost* means hard to see, but visible. Traditionally, the perfect ghost flame is one that can only be seen from certain angles and in certain light. Usually they are the same color as the base paint, only a little lighter in tone. For black base paint, you'd airbrush charcoal pearl for the ghost flames. **See fig. 26.** For a candy-blue base coat, a light-blue pearl. The reason for using pearl instead of a solid color is that pearl dusts on with nice, even coverage, whereas solid colors can

break up and appear spotty. Plus, pearl has that shimmery effect that makes it very effective for ghost flames. Ghost flames are best done over either pearl or metallic base coats, or under candy or pearl colors. A neat trick is to do a reverse of the color order above—use a dark color for the ghost flame on a lighter-color base. For example, a black ghost flame on a dark-blue candy base coat looks wicked cool.

Another clever idea is to mix a few ghost flames under a regular-flame paint job. It's easy enough to do, just follow either of the tape-off methods above, and then heavily reduce or thin down the material you are using for the flames. Here, it's especially smart to do a test panel first, to see just how much paint you need to be airbrushing and how fast you need to move the airbrush. Then, with your airbrush at low pressure, very lightly spray the edges of the tape. Pull a small bit of the tape up to check your line; the fainter or lighter the line, the better. After the tape edges are sprayed, dust on some base coat clear to seal down the pearl.

27

Aaron Stevenson

ALMOST-GHOST, MULTILAYER FLAMES
These flames aren't solid, but have too much color to be true ghost flames. **See fig. 27.** Because of this, though, they can be done on solid colors using solid colors. Here, I'm trying for an effect somewhere between a real flame and a traditional flame.

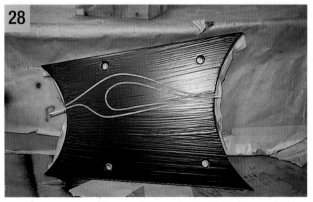

28

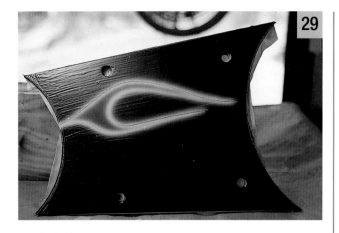

Apply four coats of Spray Mask. Once it is dry, use 1/16-inch fine line to lay out a flame. **See fig. 28.** Then cut along the edges and peel out the material.

Using a yellow-and-white-mix base coat heavily reduced, *lightly* spray along the edges. **See fig. 29.**

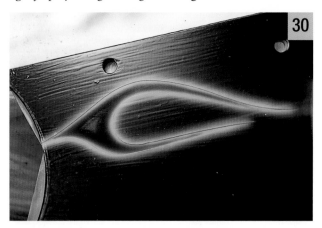

Next, spray the inside of the flame with candy orange concentrate or dye mixed with base coat clear. **Fig. 30.**

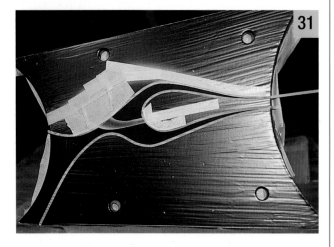

Repeat the above, but only tape off the parts of the first flame that don't cross into the new one. **Fig. 31.**

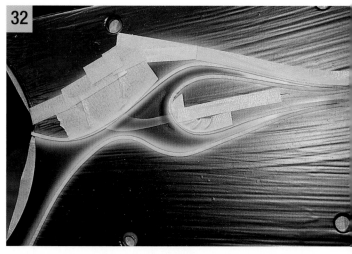

Keep repeating the process until all the layers are done. **Fig. 32.**

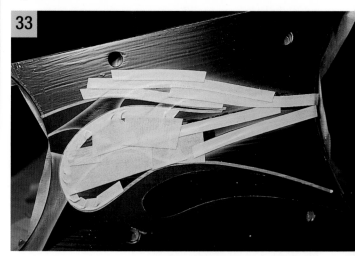

Now the third layer goes on. **Fig. 33.**

The finished primary plate in place. **Fig. 34.**

Tank featuring three layers of airbrushed flames.

35

black. I find a soft shadow is more effective than a dark one. See Chapter 7 for more details and photos.

MISCELLANEOUS FLAME TIPS

In the event there is a very heavy paint edge, look at it closely. If it sticks up too high, a flap of paint may have formed. This will need to be trimmed away with a very sharp razor blade. Just lay the blade edge flat on the surface and carefully trim the edge down. Don't worry if you mess up the edge of the flame. You can always go back after the first round of clear coat, tape off that edge, and retouch it with the airbrush. In fact, that's what I do a lot—in most of the jobs I do, I have to go back and redo a few lines here and there. It's no biggie, so don't sweat it if you see mistakes.

36

When shading the edges of airbrushed flames, sometimes overspray from the darker color can settle in the center of the flame and cause a mottled effect. To help combat this, before shading the flame, spray some base coat or Intercoat Clear over the flame center prior to edging them. This smoothes the surface, and the overspray won't tend to land there.

DOUBLE FLAMES

Very simply stated, a double-flame technique is just like any other flame style, except more sets of flames are added. **See fig. 35.** And to give them a truly three-dimensional effect, parts of each set must be taped off in order for the flames to overlap and intertwine.

Pick the flame parts that will be overlapped and tape them off. The example seen here starts by concentrating the airbrush on the center portions of the flame and spraying as little material as possible along the edges. This will result in less of a paint edge and minimize the problem of a lighter under coat peeking out around the edges of the flames. Then, take a darker candy color and spray along the edge of the flames, softly fading the color toward the middle of the flame.

Where the flames overlap, add a light black shadow using very-reduced

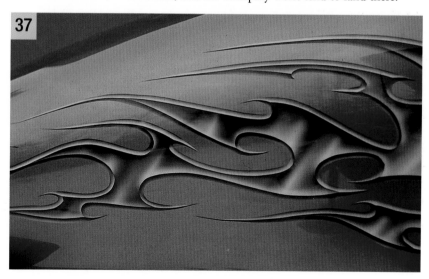

37

Close up of metal-effect tribal flames.

38

Finished result of fender seen in first example.

You may notice that on the surface where the tape was run, you can see impressions of the tape. What I do is lightly wet sand the entire area that was not flamed with 800 or 1,000 grit. This will remove these lines and any other overspray or foreign objects that have settled onto the surface.

39

Example of flame not needing to be pinstriped. Silver trimmed top edge of blue pearl flame, as done in second step-by-step, gives dimension to flames.

Close up of almost ghost flames.

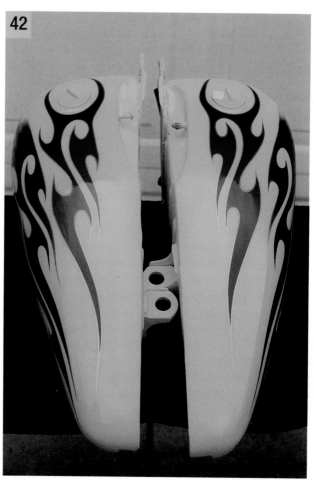

Perfectly matching tribal flame tanks.

Mixing traditional flame and pinstripe outline flame.

43

45

Sleek tribal flames on Honda UTX tank.

Two layers of solid flames and two layers of pinstriped flames.

Example of balanced flame layout on saddlebags.

44

CHAPTER 7
FLAMING A FRAME

MATERIAL AND EQUIPMENT

- House of Kolor KK-04 Oriental Blue Kandy Koncentrate
- House of Kolor KK-10 Purple Kandy Koncentrate
- White base coat tinted with purple
- White base coat tinted with blue
- Metalflake Company Spray Mask
- 1/16" and 1/8" 3M green Fine Line Tape
- 1/4", 3/4", and 2" masking tape
- Intercoat, base coat, or urethane clear
- Reducer
- Iwata HP-C airbrush
- Iwata Micron C airbrush
- Satagraph 2 airbrush
- X-acto No. 4 Stencil Knife
- Uncle Bill's Sliver Gripper tweezers
- 2x4 wooden blocks
- 4x4 wooden blocks

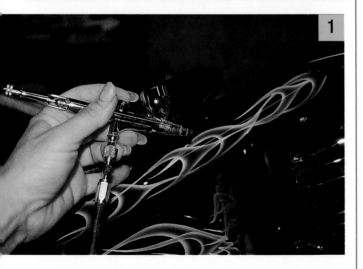

1

The biggest challenge in doing artwork on frames is the tubular shape of the frame. It's hard to find a place to steady your hand as you draw or cut or airbrush, which can result in shaky lines or uneven shading. I steady my hand by placing a finger on the frame. I use short, smooth strokes with the airbrush, only working on one flame at a time. Many times I hold the frame with one hand and lean on it with my other to help support it as I work. For example, I'm left-handed, so with my right hand, I'll lightly hold onto the frame below where I'm working. Then I'll rest my left arm on top of my right arm, and it helps steady my left hand. I also build up a support of 2x4 pieces to use in areas like the front of the downtubes, where there is nothing to lean my hands against.

It can also be a challenge to get tape to lie flat. If I'm using tape, I burnish the fine line tape down and immediately run 1/4-inch masking tape to help hold it. But in most artwork situations, I use liquid mask instead of tape. It also is essential to know what shows on a frame—no sense in doing hours of artwork on something no one will see.

I try to get fabrication photos from customers. This helps me design the best possible artwork layout for the frame. Using fabrication photos can make a huge difference in how effective the paint job is and how much time you spend doing artwork. Here I did a triple-flame paint scheme using an airbrush-faded flame technique. (More info on multiple-flame technique can be found in Chapter 6.) This example involves three tones of similar color: light blue-candy blue, and light purple-candy purple, and light magenta-candy magenta. Blue and purple always look particularly vivid when used together over a black base, and the pink or magenta intensifies the overall effect. Traditional hot-rod flames employ this technique, but use a yellow flame interior with orange and red faded along the edge. Make sure you read through Chapter 6 before attempting to paint flames on a frame—there you'll find information essential for successful flames.

2

Apply four layers of Spray Mask after bordering off the design areas with 3/4-inch masking tape. **See fig. 2.** Using a white pencil, draw the flames. I use different colored pencils for each set of flames. Take care when figuring out the overlaps. Note how the flames start at the neck and travel smoothly down the tubes, ending right where the forward controls will bolt on. **See fig. 3.**

Here, the three sets of drawn-out flames run along the seat area.

With the No. 4 knife, carefully cut out the flames, but make sure you don't cut where the flame will be overlapped by the second set. **See fig. 4.** Look closely at the picture. Cutting through the overlap is the most common mistake that will be made on this style of flame. Use the tweezers to pull off the excess material.

In order to airbrush places like the lower frame rails, raise up the frame with wooden blocks. **See fig. 5.** You'll have to move the blocks around as you airbrush in order to reach all the areas. You can see here that I placed the frame on 4x4s, then used 2x4s placed under the transmission-mounting area and under the lower rails. I could have used the front motor mount to prop up the frame, but using the

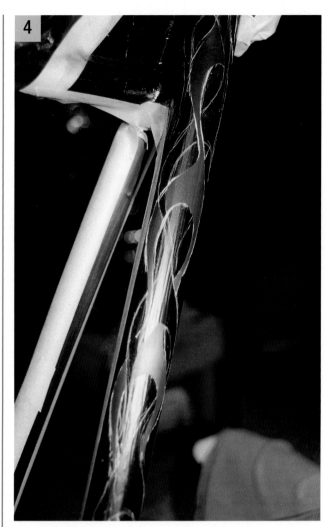

frame rails keeps the weight of the frame more evenly balanced and the frame more secure as I handled it.

Use masking paper to protect the other parts of the frame. The area covered by the gas tank is papered off. However, with some custom bikes, particularly those with a tall up stretch, that area is visible, so you may want to flame that area.

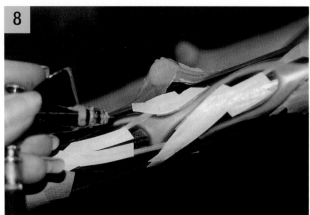

With the lighter blue, airbrush the interior of the flame, fading it out toward the edges. Then with the blue candy, airbrush along the edges, fading it toward the middle. Now, very carefully using the tweezers, peel away the next layer of flame. **See fig. 6.** Keep the No. 4 knife handy to cut bits of stencil that are still attached.

Tape off the first flame, using fine line tape. **See fig. 7.**

Now mask off the rest of the first flame, using masking tape.

Repeat the previous process, applying the lighter color in the interior of the flame. **See fig. 8.**

Edge the flame with the candy color. You can see here where the paint spit out of the airbrush and caused dark spots. **See fig. 9.**

I remedied this by airbrushing a bit of light purple over the spotty area. **See fig. 10.** Now continue your purple candy shading. I used a thicker purple for the edges and a

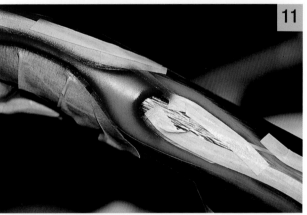

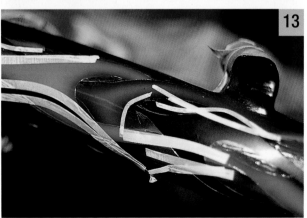

thinner purple candy for over all shading of the flame.

The purple and blue flames are done. Now cut out the magenta flames. **See fig. 12.**

Begin by taping off the blue and purple flames. **See fig. 13.**

Here you can see the neck is taped off and ready to spray. **See fig. 14.** Now I repeat the whole process, using the magenta.

I am careful to protect the frame from overspray as I work my way around. I loosely tape masking paper over the areas I'm not working on. **See fig. 15.** As I move around, I move the paper to accommodate my airbrushing. As you can see, only one rail of the frame is uncovered.

At this point, if you want, spray a few light coats of base or Intercoat Clear. Make sure it is not reduced too much. After the paint has dried for an hour or so, carefully peel away the stencil material. The amount of time to wait before removing the mask will vary, depending on how thick the paint is. Test a small area first. Pull back a little bit of mask. If the paint edge is rough and soft, with the paint on the mask not separating cleanly from the paint on the flame, wait a little longer. This is a matter of feel and observing what the paint is doing—each situation will be different. After the mask has been removed and any overspray or imperfections in the base coat sanded away, it's time to apply the first round of filler clear.

After it has dried and been sanded, I'll go back over the flames, looking for and fixing flaws, and redoing the shadows. Here you can see what the flames look like without the shadows redone. **See fig. 16.** Sorry, I had to use photos of the fender to show this part of the process. The deadline on the frame was brutal and time to take photos had run out. The flames look good, but the reshadowing process will make a huge difference.

The edge of each flame where it overlaps another flame is taped off with fine line tape, 1/16-inch for sharp curves, 3/32-inch for all other places, then 3/4-inch masking tape is run alongside it. Black is then is airbrushed along the edge. I find that this small detail can make all the difference in how dimensional the flames look, and how they "leap" from the surface. Here you can see the progression across the fender. **See fig. 17.** Some of the flames are edged with black. I've run a piece of 3/32-inch fine line tape along a flame part.

Now masking tape is laid next to it and black is softly airbrushed along the edge. **See fig. 18.**

The finished flame part is all edged with black. **See fig. 19.**

Now the inner curve of a flame is taped off and sprayed with black. **See fig. 20.** Once all the black shadow touchups are done, it's back into the booth for another round of clear.

After this round of clear, I use a clipboard with a blank sheet of paper and go over the parts, looking closely and making notes on a drawing of any flaws I find. **See fig. 21.** This sheet will help remind me of all the touchups I need

20

22

The finished product.

to make on the tank. I also did this with the frame. It's too easy to forget one spot and have your customer—or worse, your customer's nosy friends—find it at a rally somewhere in front of a crowd of people.

Basically, doing artwork on frames is not much different than doing it on sheet metal. It's just a more challenging surface to work on, due to the small diameter. There are a few other things to watch for, typical problems you encounter when flaming a frame. For example, stencil knives can slip and slice into areas not meant to be cut. The remedy is to cut very slowly. If the knife does slip, either touch up the base coat, if possible, or adjust the flame design. If there is enough clear over the base coat, you may be able to sand the cut away, but that is only a remote possibility.

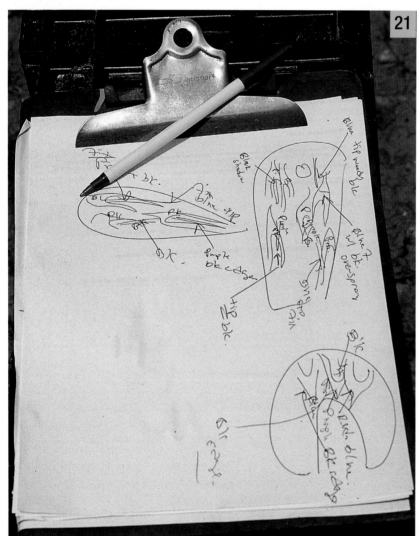

21

On the curved surface of a frame, fine line tape tends to not stay down and flat. Remedy: As quickly as possible after laying down the fine line tape, run 1/4-inch masking tape around the side of tape not being painted. This will help hold the tape down. But still, before spraying the paint, check the corners and burnish down any spots where the tape is lifting.

Frames tip over and fall all the time. Make sure the frame is well balanced, and that whatever you're using to prop it up is solid and steady. Give it a shake to test its balance to make sure you won't be busy with airbrush in hand as the frame falls away.

If the entire surface of the frame is getting artwork, the frame will need to be placed on its side for much of the artwork process. Make sure the surface it is on is freshly papered off and clean, and that it won't scratch your artwork on the other side.

When using wooden blocks to position a frame, wrap them in several layers of masking paper. The wood can scratch the paint, and paint on the blocks can rub off on the surface. Always be certain that whatever fixtures or jigs you use to hold the frame will not damage the surface.

Another flamed frame. Only two sets of flames here. Aaron Stevenson

73

CHAPTER 8
TRIBAL GRAPHICS AND OTHER GAMES

MATERIAL AND EQUIPMENT

- Tracing Paper
- Lead pencil
- MetalFlake Company's Spray Mask
- 1/8" and 1/2" 3M green Fine Line Tape
- 3/4" masking tape
- Silver pearl or any metallic paint
- White base coat
- Black base coat
- Base coat or urethane clear
- Iwata HP-C airbrush
- Iwata Micron C airbrush
- Satagraph 2 airbrush
- 2" cheap paint brush
- Ruler
- X-acto No. 4 Stencil Knife
- Uncle Bill's Sliver Grippers
- Light table or window
- Seamstress measuring tape (soft tape like used in sewing)

Spray mask used to stencil design.

Designing and painting graphics used to be so hard for me. I wondered how other artists came up with their ideas, because it always seemed so difficult. Where did they find those great designs? How did they figure out the painting technique that absolutely brought it to life? I analyzed every tribal design I could find—paintwork, tattoos—and kept a file. Tribal designs are among my favorites, and the range of ideas is endless.

I have included a few styles of tribal in this chapter, but the step-by-step follows a design made up of lines crossing each other. It's very simple, yet very effective. And the tricks seen here can be used with any type of design, not just tribals or graphics. As for airbrushing technique, I use what I call a "metal-effect" technique that gives the design a three-dimensional, metallic feel. This technique can be used with any design, from a larger area graphic to a dagger tribal design to flames.

Here the surface is masked off with Spray Mask. Start out by covering the parts with Spray Mask, using 3/4-inch masking tape to border off the areas where the graphic will go. With a 2-inch paint brush, apply four coats of Spray Mask, allowing each coat to dry before applying the next. It will dry to a transparent, bluish color. **See fig. 2.** Take tracing paper and wrap it around the tank or fender—you may have to tape two pieces together to make it fit. Now draw out the design you want. I use this tracing-paper technique so I don't have five different designs on the surface of the tank or fender to confuse me.

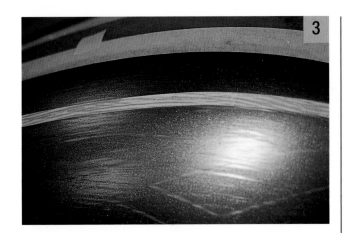

3

Use 1/8-inch green fine line tape to help get the lines straight. **See fig. 3.** Just run tape along the lines, then trace along the tape. To get the lines even and perfectly spaced, use various sizes of masking or fine line tape between the strips. Here I ran 1/2-inch masking tape along my lines, using the tape for spacing, and traced along the tape. Now I have perfectly spaced, uniform lines. I run fine line tape to help trace a nice even taper to the end.

4

Mark each line to show where it will overlap another line, using an "O" for overlap and a "U" for underlap. **See fig. 4.**

To design the top of the tank, make a copy of the original tracing and lay it down next to a blank sheet of paper. **See fig. 5.** Draw a line down the center of the blank paper. Now just transfer the lines by redrawing them on the blank paper. Here my original had a curve to it because the tank side had a curve, but I needed a straight design on the top of the tank, so I had to redraw the design to be straight. This new, straight design can also be used on the fenders. Just reduce the size using a photocopier, or lengthen the ends by drawing them longer. You can also load the design into a computer and use a graphics program (even MSPaint) to manipulate the drawing into whatever size or shape you need. After the drawing is done, flip it over, and using a light table or window, trace along the lines with a *lead* pencil. (You'll see why shortly.)

5

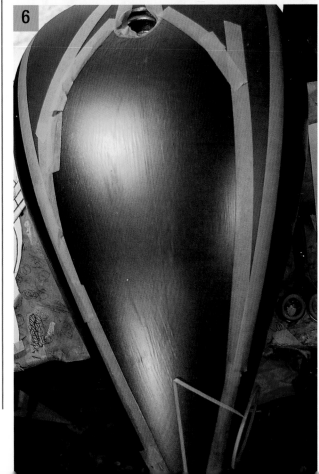

6

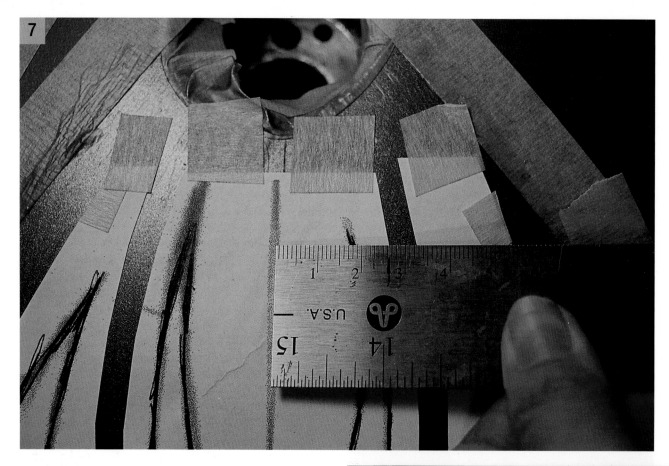

Next, using 1/8-inch tape, find the center of the tank and lay down the tape. **See fig. 6.** Draw a line down both sides of it. Then remove the tape.

To line up the centerline of the drawing and tank, simply place the line of the drawing on the center of the two lines on the tank. **See fig. 7.** In this case, I found that my top drawing wasn't quite wide enough for the space. So I cut it into three sections and spaced them equally apart, using a ruler to measure each space.

Measure from the center to the side of the cut part, then make a mark to line up and space the other side accurately. **See fig. 8.** Once the design is in place to your satisfaction, trace

along the lines with a pen and the pencil lead on the opposite side of the paper will leave the design on the mask material.

Use tape to evenly redraw the sides of the lines. **See fig. 9.** That's why my lines look so even. Run 1/2-inch tape alongside the 1/8-inch fine line.

For the tapered ends, run 1/8-inch tape from the point to where the line will stop tapering—the point where you already spaced the line with the thicker tape. **See fig. 10.**

10

11

12

panic. Just keep working, and after the first round of clear coat, retouch it. The clear will fill the cut line and the rework will be completely hide the mistake.

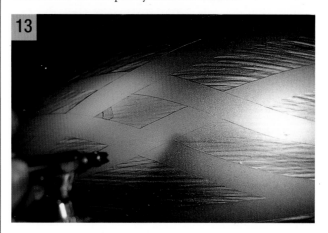

13

Airbrush a few layers of silver pearl or any metallic over the design, just enough to cover. **See fig. 13.** Don't overdo it, or you'll end up with a thick paint edge.

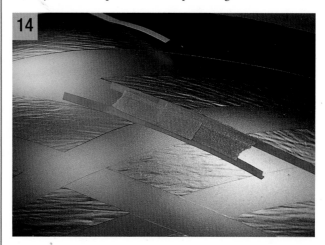

14

The top design all laid out and ready for cutting. **See fig. 11.** Use great care when cutting out the design—because of the overlaps. You don't want to cut through them. **See fig. 12.** If you do, it will leave a cut impression in a place where there is no line. That's why the Os and Us are used. If you do end up cutting through a place you didn't intend, don't

Now comes the tricky part. You have to tape off each line so it can be airbrushed separately, but you also need to tape off each overlap on the line. Tape off the overlaps first. **See fig. 14.**

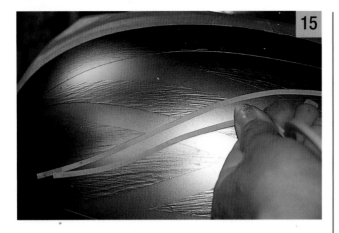

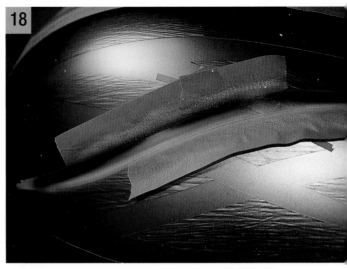

Because the lines will have airbrushed edges, use 1/8-inch fine line tape and run it along the *inside* of the lines. **Fig. 15.**

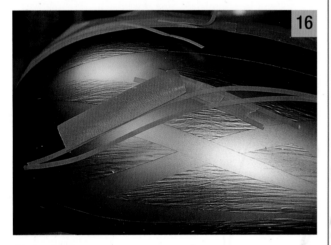

Airbrush some black at the top edge. **See fig. 17.** Airbrush some white along the bottom edge. **See fig. 18.**

Use 3/4-inch masking tape alongside the fine line, but bend up the edges so they form a "spraybreak," which deflects overspray away from the other design surfaces. **Fig. 16.**

Pull away the fine line tape. Then, using fine line tape and masking tape, tape off the top half and airbrush black along the top edge and white along the bottom edge. **See fig. 19.** Now tape off the bottom line and repeat, reversing the colors. Try to imagine how the light would hit the lines if they were actually three-dimensional— what would be in darkness and where the light would reflect.

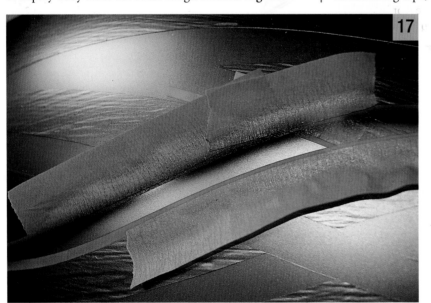

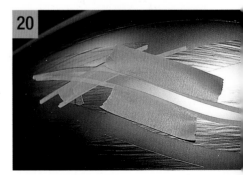

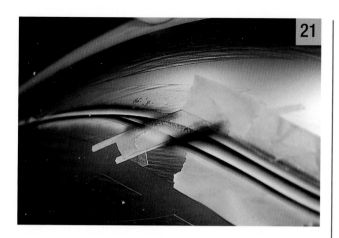

Now tape off another line. **See fig. 20.**

At the overlaps, airbrush some thinned black. **See fig. 21.** You don't want the black to be grainy. You just want a slight shadow.

For the pointed ends, run fine line tape from the point of the inner line to the point of the cutout line. **Fig. 22.**

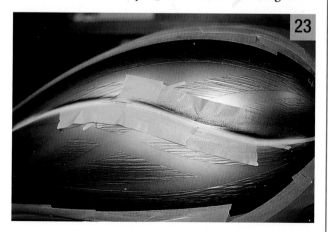

Tape it off and spray white along the tape, running it along the bottom edge of the taped-off area. **Fig. 23.**

Pull away the tape to reveal the crisp, white edge. Note that the three-dimensional effect is already starting. **Fig. 24.**

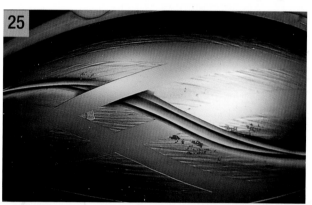

Completed line. **See fig. 25.**

Now to airbrush a "dagger" line. Run the 1/8-inch tape along the inner edges. **See fig. 26.** Notice how it crosses at the inner point.

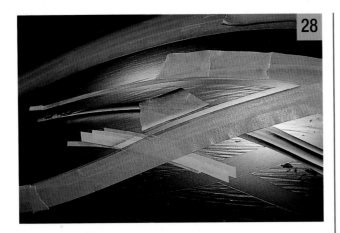

Simply cut or trim the ends away, leaving a point. **See fig. 27.** Now airbrush the black and white.

Now tape off the 1/8-inch edges. **See fig. 28.**

Aaron Stevenson

Run a piece of tape across, from point to point, forming the hard edge. **See fig. 29.** Spray black to shadow. Reverse tape it and spray white underneath.

The finished tank.

Completed sharp corner of the dagger line. This black-and-white process is actually fairly simple, and achieves a great metal effect. **See fig. 30.** It's easy, too—if only if all paint jobs were this much fun.

Completed side of the tank. **Fig 31.**

Now peel away the mask. Carefully pull backward, breaking the paint seal. Cut the mask apart as you go, so that it comes off in pieces. This way you pull up each part of the mask individually, as if it were tape, so that it comes up cleanly and leaves a crisp edge to the graphic.

Check out the following pictures. This silver-white-black method goes great with any color, especially those odd colors that are difficult to mate with suitable contrasting graphic colors. Candy toners or colored tints could be added to get a colored-metal effect. There are no hard or fast rules here. Take the methods you see and play with them—experiment and have fun.

33

Another view showing tank top.

34

Tribal skull design also done with Spray Mask. Big skull was airbrushed with frisket paper stencils and paper stencils, which were also used for the little skulls.

Now you'll notice that on the surface where the tape was run, you can see impressions from the tape. What I do is lightly wet sand the entire area that was not airbrushed with 1,000 grit, removing these lines and any other overspray or foreign objects that have settled onto the surface. After that, go to Chapter 15.

35

Three layers of graphics. Each layer was taped off with fine line and masking tape and sprayed individually.

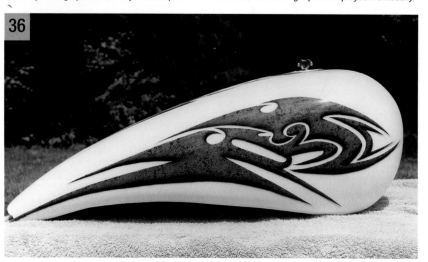

36

This tribal was also laid out with Spray Mask. The color was applied by dabbing sponges in paint and then dabbing them on the design, then the bottom edges were lightly airbrushed in black.

37

Both the flames and the metal-effect razor graphics were drawn out at the same time on Spray Mask. First the flames were cut out and sprayed. Next, the graphics were cut out and the flames masked off. Then the graphics were sprayed.

38

39

This Road King graphic ties into the bags from the rear fender. It was all done with fine line tape. First the stripe areas were covered with 1/2-inch green fine line and the teal pearl, then teal candy was faded with an airbrush over the black. Then the stripes were taped off and softly airbrushed with purple. A black edge running along one side of the stripes adds dimension.

Another design done with Spray Mask, using the same metal-effect technique as seen in the step-by-step with flames and razor graphics.

CHAPTER 9
LUSCIOUS LIQUID GRAPHICS

MATERIAL AND EQUIPMENT

- Tracing Paper
- MetalFlake Company's Spray Mask
- 1/8" 3M green Fine Line Tape
- 3/4" masking tape
- Graphix frisket paper
- Any color base coat with light and dark tones (candy) mixed up
- Iwata HP-C airbrush
- Iwata Micron C airbrush
- Satagraph 2 airbrush
- 2" cheap paint brush
- Ruler
- X-acto No. 4 Stencil Knife
- Uncle Bill's Sliver Grippers
- Light table or window
- Seamstress measuring tape (soft tape used in sewing)
- Lead pencil

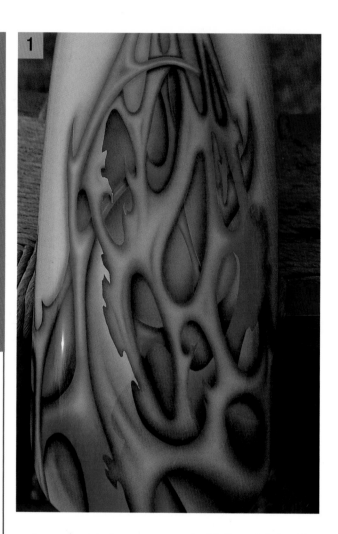

One of the simplest methods for doing killer graphics is what I call a liquid technique. It's basically overlapping lines that resemble a liquid. Liquid graphics can be one simple layer or extreme multilayers. Either way, the possibilities are endless.

Have fun with this technique, because it's hard to make mistakes doing these graphics. If you screw up, just rework your design to allow for the mistake and no one will even notice—it might even look better. There have been times when I had to rework a design to allow for a boo-boo and ended up with a better design.

Start out with the parts covered with Spray Mask, using 3/4-inch masking tape to border off the areas you want the graphic. **See fig. 2.** With a 2-inch paint brush, apply four coats of Spray Mask, allowing each coat to dry before applying the next. It will dry to a transparent bluish color.

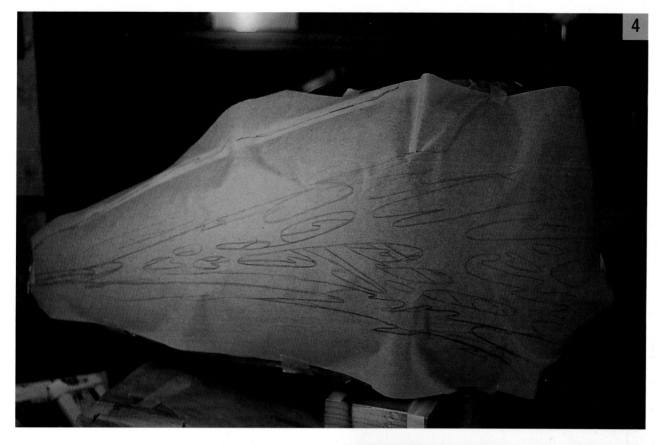

Now take tracing paper and wrap it around the tank or fender. **See fig. 3.** You may need to tape two pieces together to make it fit. Draw out the design you want. Use 1/8-inch green fine line tape to help get the lines straight—just run tape along where a straight line is needed and trace it.

This drawing is finished. **See fig. 4.** Put reference marks on the tank and paper so the paper can be replaced in the exact same location after you complete the next step. Remove the paper, flip it over, and using a light table or window, trace along the design with a lead pencil.

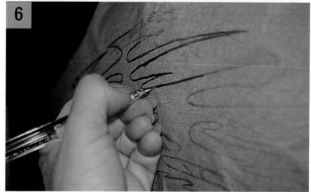

Now replace the paper on the tank. **See fig. 5.**

With a pencil, trace along the lines, leaving an outline of the design on the tank. **See fig. 6.** Use a white Stabilo pencil to retrace the design on the tank. This makes it more visible and allows you to rework the design in a few places.

8

The design is now all drawn out in white pencil. **Fig 7.** For places where the design lines need to be absolutely straight, run 1/8-inch fine line tape along the line and trace that. **See fig. 8.**

9

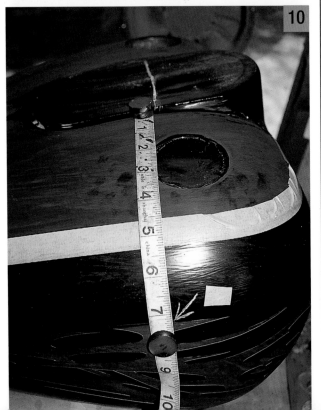

10

Using a #4 knife, cut out the design. **See fig. 9.** To reproduce the design on the other side, flip the drawing over, then pick a few reference points on the cutout design and measure from points at the top of the tank.

Use the seam that runs down the middle of the tank or the dash area for a reference point; for fenders, I use the center of the fender. **See fig. 10.** Next, simply measure on the other side down to the reference points.

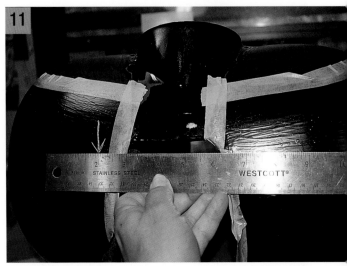

11

Do the same thing at the front of the tank. **See fig. 11.**

12

Put an arrow at the end of the liquid line, measure from the front seam, and make a corresponding mark on the other side. **See fig. 12.**

Line up the drawing to trace the design from on the other side. **See fig. 13.** Refer to Chapters 5 and 13 for exact details on reproducing the design on the other side of the tank. Then using a No. 4 stencil knife, lightly cut out the design, but don't cut down too hard. Cut only through the spray mask and not into the paint. Use sliver tweezers to pull up the stencil, keeping the knife handy to cut off any bits that are still attached.

Sometimes part of the stencil may inadvertently get pulled up. **See fig. 14.** Trim away the mask as planned, including the pulled-up part. **See fig. 15.**

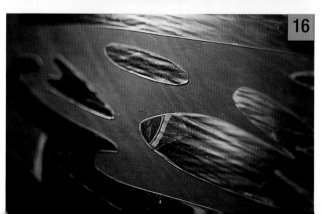

Take a small piece of frisket paper and apply it to the area. Then trim it out in the shape the stencil was supposed to be. **See fig. 16.**

In some cases, you can use the heel end of the tweezers to seal down stencil parts that lift. **See fig. 17.**

Airbrush the lighter color first, using a thinned-down light blue. **See fig. 18.**

In areas where the liquid will overlap itself, tape off the part of the design that will go "under" the liquid. **See fig. 19.** Concentrate the paint toward the middle of those areas,

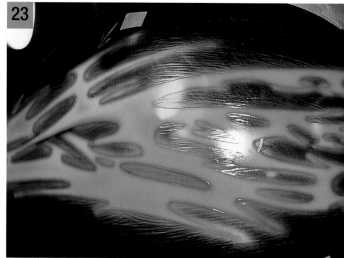

and try to create a rounded, three-dimensional effect by leaving the edges darker.

After the light blue is done, airbrush around the edges with a thinned-down candy blue and try to imagine the "hollows" that can form in the liquid. **See fig. 20.** Airbrush those in the big areas where the lines come together. Think about the way liquid pulls its surface as you spray the darker color.

For the overlap areas, just tape it off, spray the darker color, and spray some black as shadow. **See fig. 21.**

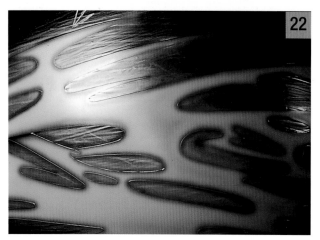

Work your way around the design, gradually building up color. **See fig. 22.**

Imagine places where the liquid pools and sags. Softly airbrush darker tones there. **See fig. 23.** Bang! You're done. Let it dry for an hour or so, depending on how much paint you applied. Always pull tape or stencil material back and away from itself, breaking the paint line. Never pull directly up. If it looks like the paint is pulling away with the stencil, use a stencil knife to carefully slice the paint from the stencil *before* you pull the stencil away.

Now you'll notice that on the surface, at the places where the tape was run, you can see impressions of the tape. **See fig. 24.** What I do is I lightly wet sand the entire area (that was *not* airbrushed) with 1,000 grit, removing these lines and any other overspray or foreign objects that have settled onto the surface. OK, now it's time for filler clear coats: Refer to Chapter 15 for filler clear coating details.

23

Here the finished artwork is ready for clear.

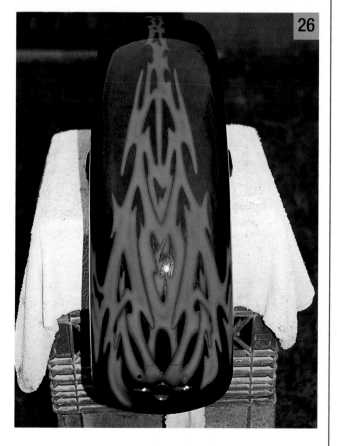

26

Finished!

27

Fun and games with spray mask: I drew on the webbing, then bit by bit, cut it away and airbrushed the web. It's a good thing I had a drawing to refer to. Spray mask used to stencil design.

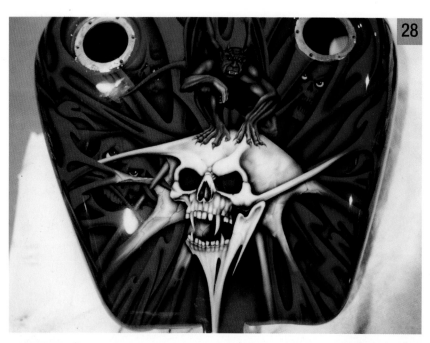

28

The end result.

29

30

I had no idea this webbing would be so cool-looking. The cross was done with regular frisket paper after I applied tons of clear coat over the webbed base to protect it.

Just another example of less is more. Aaron Stevenson

31

This graphic complements the lines of the fender. Aaron Stevenson

The graphic travels across the parts.

Aaron Stevenson

CHAPTER 10
GOLD, SILVER, AND VARIEGATED METAL LEAF

MATERIAL AND EQUIPMENT

- Mona Lisa Varigated Red Metal Leaf (any color or kind of leaf can be used)
- Mona Lisa Gold Leaf Adhesive Size
- HOK AP-01 Adhesion Promoter
- 1/16", 1/8", and 1/2" 3M green Fineline tape
- 3/4" masking tape
- Squirrel hair lettering brush
- Scissors
- Tracing paper
- Steel ruler
- Piece of velvet cloth

"Gold leaf is some tedious stuff. I hate working with it. How do you handle it without it breaking apart?" I hear this from painters all the time. But with a little patience and a little knowledge, doing metal leaf work can be fun.

I really like working with it. I like to use silver leaf under candy paint. For this step-by-step, I'm applying a variegated metal leaf design on a single downtube frame. The tricks in this chapter for putting artwork on a single downtube frame can be used with any other artwork technique, as well. Metal leaf comes in several colors: green, black, blue, and red. The parts I'm using are painted with HOK Kandy Wild Cherry, so I'll use the red leaf.

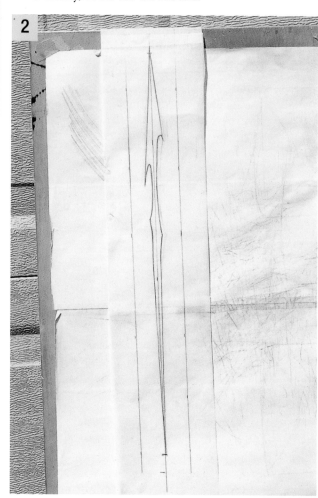

Silver leaf pinstripes were applied over a silver Marblized base, and then candy tangerine was applied.

First, I measure the width of the downtube. Then I draw the tube using that measurement on a long piece of tracing paper with a centerline down the middle. **See fig. 2.** Next I draw my design out on it, flip the paper over, and trace along the design.

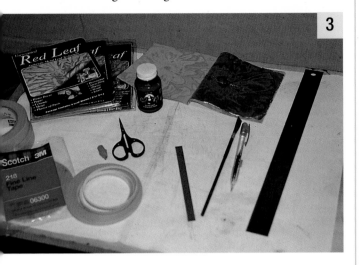

Now I gather up the stuff I'll need to do the leaf work. **See fig. 3.** From left to right, clockwise: variegated red leaf, adhesive size, steel rulers, mechanical pencil, squirrel hair lettering brush, scissors, green fine line tape, and masking tape.

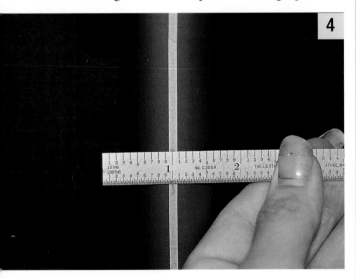

Find the center of the downtube. I usually do this by eye, laying 1/8-inch green fine line tape along the center. Then with a steel ruler, I eyeball-measure from the center of the tape to the sides of the tube. **See fig. 4.** Since the frame is on a table, I get down below it and sight up the tube, making sure the tape is straight. If I find any bumps in the line of the tape, I mark those spots with tape and rerun the 1/8-inch tape.

The centerline of the drawing is lined up with the center of the tape and taped into place. **See fig. 5.** Slots are cut in the paper in several places so it can wrap around the tube

smoothly. The portions of the fine line tape on the tube onto which the line of the design crosses are carefully pulled up and removed.

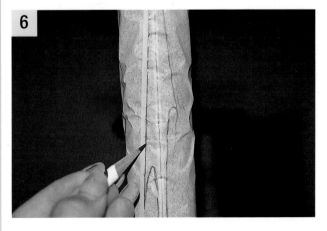

Trace along the lines to transfer the design to the frame. **See fig. 6.** I run 1/8-inch fine line along the straight lines to help keep them straight.

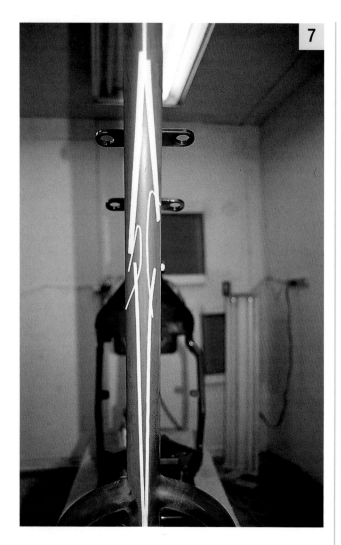

Then tape off the design with fine line tape. **See fig.** 7. I use 1/16-inch where the lines have a sharp curve. The fine line is bordered with 3/4-inch masking tape.

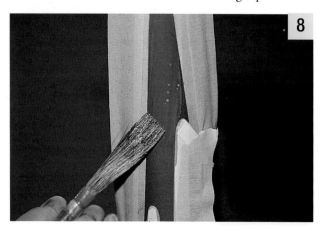

Brush on a thin, even layer of size. **See fig. 8.** Before you begin, make sure the brush is very clean, and then after the size is applied, wash the brush immediately in soapy water.

As the adhesive dries, it will change from milky white to clear. When it is completely clear, it is ready for leaf application. This sometimes takes an hour, but my shop was very hot that day, and it dried in 15 minutes.

The leaf tears very easily! It helps to sandwich a sheet of leaf between two pieces of tracing paper and cut it into strips that will fit the space where it will go. **See fig. 9.**

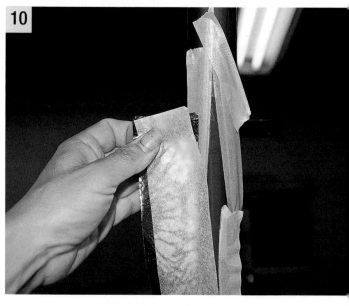

Now here's the tricky part: Hold the leaf just above where you will place it, let the bottom sheet of paper drop away, and place the leaf onto the surface. **See fig. 10.** Any movement of air in the shop will blow the leaf sheet around, so make sure no fan is on.

Smooth the leaf on the design surface by softly smoothing the tracing paper on the **See fig. 11.** Don't press too hard—as I said, it tears very easy. Use a fingernail to burnish the leaf into the corners, up against the tape edge. You can also use a piece of velvet to smooth the surface and burnish

the leaf onto the surface, but I always start out working on top of the tracing paper. Once the leaf has taken hold, I then wrap a piece of velvet cloth around a fingertip and gently but firmly smooth down the leaf. Very softly, keep smoothing back and forth until the surface looks very metallike and very flat. If the leaf crumples against the sized surface, just pull off the leaf that didn't stick, and carefully place other strips of leaf around what is there. Don't lose patience with this process. Once you get the hang of handling the leaf, it's a breeze.

HANDY HINT

Before the tape or stencil is removed, to get that classic effect when doing real gold leaf, place a wad of fabric onto the end of a round wooden dowel or stick. Then wrap a piece of velvet around the wad, securing it with tape around the handle of the stick. Now, put the velvet pad against the surface of the leaf and give it a gentle twist. Move it over just a bit and give it another turn. Keep repeating this process along the surface of the leaf, and you'll create authentic soft swirls.

At this point there will be places where the leaf will overlap itself. Make sure you remove the extra leaf in those areas by lightly brushing the extra leaf away with your very clean fingers. Don't overdo it with heavy fingers when you touch the leaf! Closely look over the surface and make sure all the loose bits of leaf are wiped away—this is very important! Bubbles can form under loose leaf, so go over the surface carefully.

Now with the airbrush, apply two light coats of House of Kolor Adhesion Promoter AP-10. Then apply two light coats of base coat or Intercoat Clear. *Don't skip this step, or the paint may not stick to the leaf.* Peel away the tape or stencil.

This is what I have so far. See where size has snuck past the tape? **See fig. 12.**

The unwanted size is carefully wiped off with precleaner and a folded paper towel. **See fig. 13.** Don't touch the leaf. It's ready for around of clear. If you're working over base

coat clear, use base coat clear. If working over urethane clear, use that. Do not use base coat clear over urethane, as that can in some cases result in adhesion problems.

Once that is applied, dried, and wet sanded, I'll pinstripe it. It could be pinstriped freehand before clear coating, but then the edge of the metal leaf might show through the stripe, so wait until after you've cleared. If this is your first time

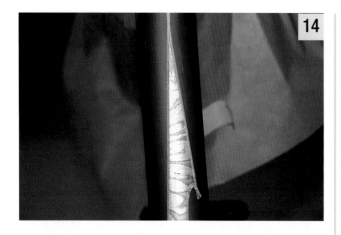

doing leaf work, I strongly advise you to do a test piece first. Different brands of paint react to leaf in different ways, so play around and make sure the paint sticks to the leaf.

Once the clear has been sanded, tape a pinstripe and airbrush it. This method of tape-off pinstriping can only be done over urethane clear, as the frisket will stick too well to base coat paint and end up leaving lots of the adhesive behind. I border the design with 1/16-inch green fine line tape, taping the tight corners last. **See fig. 14.** I'll deal with those first, as the tape tends to pull up there.

I cut out small pieces of frisket paper and stick them in areas that are difficult to tape, like the insides of the pointed ends and the insides and outsides of the tight curves. **See fig. 15.** Press the frisket in tightly against the tape edge, using a fingernail.

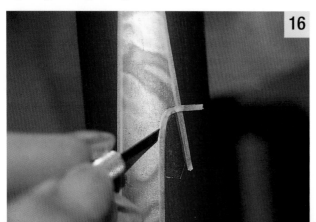

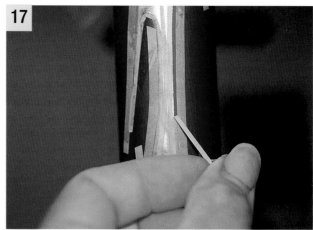

Cut along the 1/16-inch tape with a No. 4 knife and use tweezers to pull up the cutout frisket. **See fig. 16.**

Lay down 1/8-inch (along the straights and slight curves) and 1/16-inch fine line (for the narrow spaces and tight curves) along the edges of the first piece of 1/16-inch tape that you laid down. Keep it straight and as tight to the edge as possible. Take care when overlapping the frisket and tape, or paint will sneak underneath at that junction. Pull up the first 1/16-inch tape. **See fig. 17.**

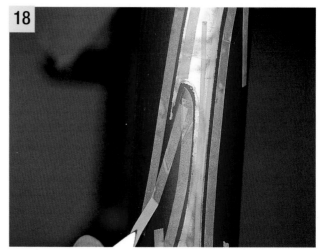

Bring the ends of the 1/8-inch tape together to form points on the ends. **See fig. 18.**

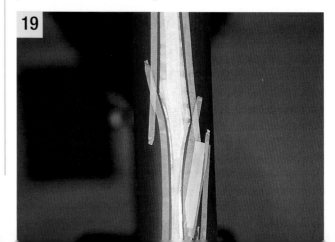

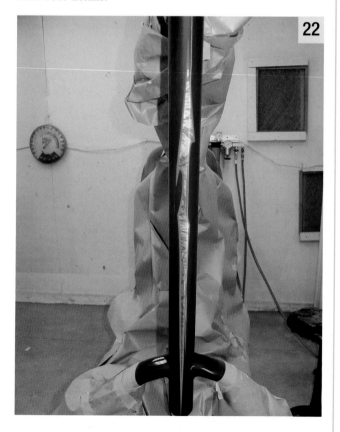

20

Now it's ready for paint. **See fig. 19.**

Using an airbrush, spray on two to three coats of paint. House of Kolor Molly Orange is used here. Don't go too heavy, or there'll be a thick paint edge. After a few minutes, pull the tape away, pulling it back against itself—never pull tape directly up. Check for adhesive where the frisket was used, and use precleaner with a folded paper towel to remove any remaining adhesive, but don't touch the pinstripe. Now apply clear, but make sure the first coats are light, as the pinstripe might run or sag if the initial clear coats are too heavy. Check out Chapter 15 for clear coat details.

22

The finished result.

23

A vinyl stencil cut on a plotter was used for this tank on the Carolina Panthers' commemorative Fatboy.

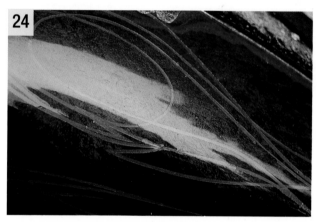

24

A close-up of silver leaf pinstripe under candy paint.

GOLD, SILVER, AND VARIEGATED METAL LEAF

CHAPTER 11
HOW TO DO A SIMPLE AIRBRUSHED MURAL

MATERIAL AND EQUIPMENT

- Grafix Frisket Paper
- Stabilo Pencils
- Lead pencil
- Base coat colors for mural
- Iwata HP-C airbrush
- Iwata Micron C airbrush
- Satagraph 2 airbrush
- X-acto No. 4 Stencil Knife
- Uncle Bill's Sliver Grippers
- Light table or window
- Magnets

People sometimes see my airbrush work and ask if it's a decal. They say it looks too realistic to have been painted on. The trick to doing realistic murals, at least for me, is to use photos for reference whenever possible. I have hundreds of photos of clouds, women, scenic views of nature—all kinds of stuff. I collect photos from nature calendars and magazines. I keep them all in files labeled "Wolves," "Eagles," and so on. I have a whole bookcase in my studio filled with photo books, everything from lions and tigers to exotic women and gargoyles. I also have extensive photo files on my computer for quick and easy reference.

Some of my favorite subjects to airbrush are clouds and storm scenes. I don't really plan them out the way I do most of my work. I do have an extensive file of cloud photos I've taken over the years, and sometimes get "in the mood" and get ideas by sifting through them, picking out a few that have elements that fit my current paint scheme, and also look like they would fit the space I'm airbrushing.

For this fender I chose a tall photo and changed the colors around, using shades of purple and blue. **See fig. 2.** This particular photo doesn't have lightning in it, but it is easy enough to imagine. I'll add the lightning later.

Since the fender is a dark color, I use a white Stabilo pencil to lightly sketch out the clouds. **See fig. 3.** Sometimes I just draw them out freehand with the airbrush. I made up two white, two very light purple, and two black base coat mixtures. One mix is more reduced than the other for lighter, less grainy shading. I also made up blue and purple candy clear base coat mixes. You can also use Intercoat Clear.

With the thicker light purple, begin to fill in the clouds. **See fig. 4.** Keep the photo close by for reference. (I'll usually put photos in a plastic bag to protect them and tape the bags right next to where I'm working.) Look at the bright spots in the clouds—the puffy, high spots—to figure out where the light is coming from, and fill those in. Airbrush along the cloud outline with a very thin, light line. The Iwata Micron works well for this. Look at some photos of lightning bolts. Lightly sketch in a few, and then highlight the cloud parts that face the lightning bolts.

Little by little, fill in clouds. **See fig. 5.**

OK, the clouds are roughed in with the light purple. It's time to add some color. **See fig. 6.**

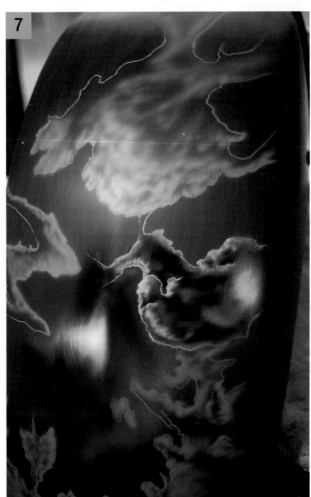

Start shading with the candy purple. **See fig. 7.** Concentrate the purple in the darker areas and fade it into the light purple.

Now it's starting to look like something. **See fig. 8.** Airbrush some blue in. Against the purple, the blue shows up as a cobalt that blends into the purple tones.

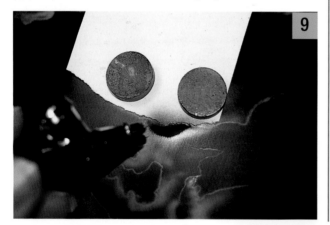

Use magnets to hold a piece of torn paper on the fender. **See fig. 9.** Then spray along the edge to give a sharp but soft edge to a cloud, creating more depth.

Close up of the detail. **See fig. 10.** The purple shadows really bring the cloud to life.

Airbrush some reduced black into the dark, shadowed areas, creating more depth in the clouds. **See fig. 11.**

Wrap the clouds around the edge of the fender, continuing the design down the side. **See fig. 12.** Once I'm done with the clouds, I clear coat over what I have. (See Chapter 15.) There are several reasons for doing this. I will be spraying lightning next, and sometimes the candy colors I use in the background can bleed into the white, muting it out. For example, on this fender, the white

lightning would turn purple and blue. I also find that when I spray the white lightning, overspray from the white tends to travel all over the fender. This way, I can remove any overspray by damp sanding. There is no problem with color bleeding through the white, and I get a nice, fresh, smooth surface to work on.

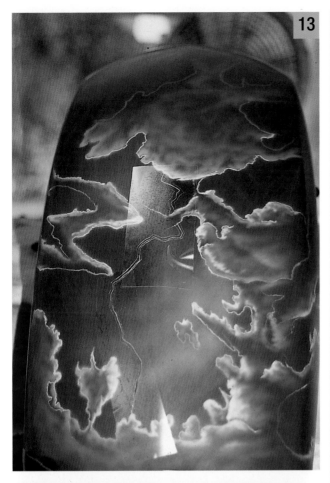

13

After clearing and sanding with 800 grit, take pieces of Grafix Frisket Paper and stick them on the fender where the lightning bolts will run. **See fig. 13.** You could also use Spray Mask or transfer tape for this.

Next, cut out the bolts with a No. 4 knife, taking care to not cut deeply into the paint surface. **See fig. 14.** The bolts start out thick at the point they leave the cloud and get thinner as they travel down. Use sliver tweezers to easily grab and pull up the cutout bolts.

15

Add a few smaller bolts coming out from below the main cloud. **See fig. 15.**

16

Airbrush the bolts with thick white, but don't use too many coats. You don't want a thick paint edge sticking up. **See fig. 16.**

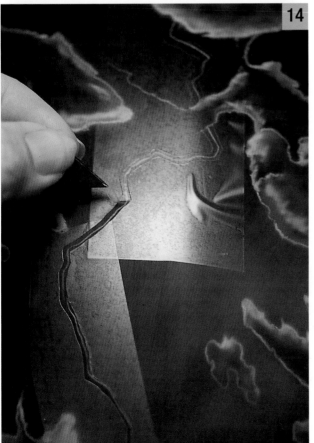

14

17

Lighter colors can be weird. Their overspray tends to stick everywhere. Even though the frisket paper didn't leave any adhesive behind, there is a slight image on the surface where it was. The white overspray will stick to this, so I lightly damp sand the area where the frisket was, using 1,000-grit paper. **See fig. 17.**

Next, I use torn paper to mask off the clouds, because I'm going to use the thinned-down white and airbrush the electric glow around each bolt. **See fig. 18.** Again, use magnets to hold the paper in place. (You could also tape it.) Now it's clear coat time. Go to Chapter 15.

The finished fender. **See fig. 19.** You can really see the blue tones in this photo.

The matching tank. **See fig. 20.**

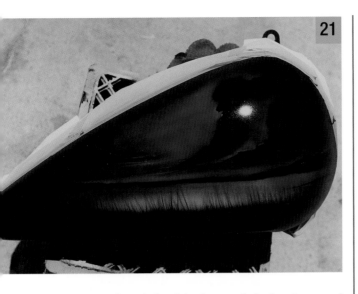

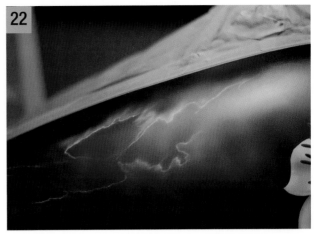

Two examples of cloud backgrounds before I sprayed foreground artwork.

Another lightning storm mural. I love the way the clouds came out on this tank.

These clouds sweep around the entire tank. The light hits them at the correct angle, which makes all the difference.

This is one of my favorite murals. **See figs. 25 and 26.** The clouds are so puffy and realistic. I worked from photos, first drawing the outline of the clouds with an airbrush using white. Light grays were softly sprayed into the dark areas of the clouds. Then I went over the outline again with white, holding the airbrush very close to the surface to get a hairline width. Highlights were applied by holding the airbrush farther away and softly "poofing" the white. The bright highlight on the upper cloud section was done by spraying white along the edge of a business card, then turning the card and spraying again. Wait a bit in between, as the card will smudge the wet paint you just applied.

One of the cool things about this mural is that it covers the whole fender. The black shadow of the top cloud turns into a starry night sky, and then morphs back into daylight.

More poofy clouds. I had fun playing with the black-to-light-blue transition. **See fig. 27.**

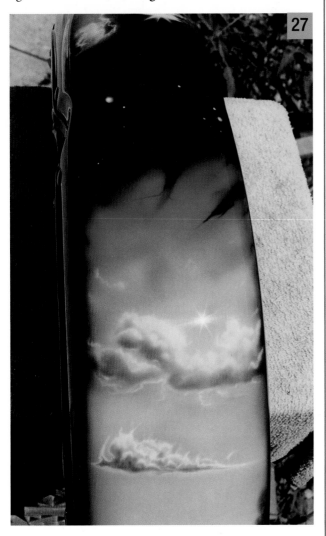

27

CHAPTER 12
AIRBRUSHING A WOLF FACE

MATERIAL AND EQUIPMENT

- Grafix Frisket Paper
- Stabilo Pencils
- Lead pencil
- Base coat colors
- White
- Black
- Dark brown mixture
- Root beer transparent toner
- Red
- Yellow
- Iwata HP-C airbrush
- Iwata Micron C airbrush
- Satagraph 2 airbrush
- X-acto No. 4 Stencil Knife (for frisket)
- X-acto No. 11 Knife (for paper)
- Uncle Bill's Sliver Grippers
- Light table or window
- Magnets

The toughest part of airbrushing any kind of animal is getting the texture of creature's surface to appear realistic. With birds I make feathery stencils to use on areas like the neck and body, and individually spray each feather on the wings. For scaly creatures like alligators, I use the plastic netting material from a bag of onions.

I seldom get the technique perfect the first time. I experiment around, trying different things until something works. Animal fur is hard because there is no trick to it. It has to be airbrushed freehand. Achieving that soft texture of light and darks and the illusion of individual hairs without the result looking rough and hairy can take some time to perfect.

Here I was working on a Fatboy tank that I had painted with a base coat of black and then sprayed with a light layer of HOK Lilac Marblizer (which I did not marblize). I then applied a few coats of candy. I used HOK Cobalt Blue mixed 1:1 with HOK Wild Cherry, then mixed with base coat clear. The reason I used the Marblizer and not regular pearl is that Marblizer is very, very fine. It has a light, soft glow that works perfectly for the effect I wanted. I wanted a dark

base coat, almost black, but I also wanted it to light up purple where the light hit it—an electric purple. But I didn't want the darkness or blackness of the base to be toned down by the candy, so I used the colored Marblizer pearl. That way I didn't need to use much candy.

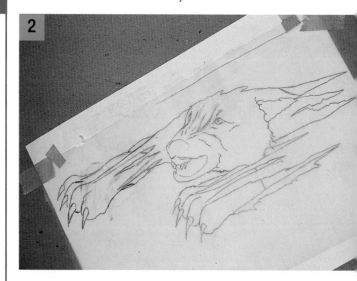

For this job the customer wanted a lightning storm mural, but also a wolf. **See fig. 2.** We came up with the idea of having a wolf tearing through the surface of the lightning storm. I'd never tried anything like this, but since I've painted many wolves and some wicked storms, I didn't think it would be too hard. I spent some time going through all my wolf books and photos, looking for wolf faces that have the same expression and the same viewing angle as the drawing I made for the customer. When I found the right ones, I made color copies of them to keep close by for reference as I airbrushed the wolf.

The surface was wet sanded with 600 grit. I'd made different sized copies of the drawing and I used the one that was 25 percent bigger than the original. This drawing was cut out and placed on the tank. **See fig. 3.** Once I found the proper placement, I lightly traced around the cutout with a pencil—I didn't want to waste time painting clouds that would be covered by the wolf. The sky was airbrushed freehand with basecoats of white, black, and a mix of purple and white. To darken the clouds, I used a base coat candy mix that matched the base paint. Refer to Chapter 11 for details on cloud painting.

Here is the sky with the wolf drawing. **See fig. 4.** At this point I applied a few rounds of urethane clear over it to protect the artwork I'd done. Plus it gave me a fresh surface to work on. While my clear was hardening, I made stencils for the ripping wolf. I simply used a light table or window to trace the wolf and the rips onto frisket paper and cut them out with a No. 4 stencil knife. I also made a few paper copies of the drawing for use as quickie stencil cut outs.

After the clear was wet sanded with 600 grit, I lined up the cutout wolf from the stencil using the pencil lines on the tank. **See fig. 5.** Then the stencil was placed around it. The stencil must be cut apart and then put in place, because the stencil is flat and the tank is round.

Here the stencil is seen on the tank. **See fig. 6.** It was time to mix up wolf colors. The best wolf mural I ever airbrushed used lots of warm tones, not just cool grays. Here, I used a medium gray, white, light tan (more white than yellow), another light tan (more yellow than white), a brown and black mixture, and very reduced black. All the colors should have two mixtures: one thicker for initial shading, and one very reduced for fine detail shading.

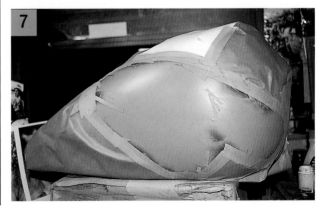

Spray the wolf with gray. **See fig. 7.** Flip the drawing over, and with a pencil trace along things like the eyes, mouth, muzzle wrinkles, nose, maybe even some of the color separations in the fur to indicate where darker airbrushing needs to be done. Now flip the drawing back over, place it within the stencil, tape it down, and trace along the same lines, transferring the lines to the paint surface.

Now with the reference photo nearby, airbrush along those lines. **See fig. 8.** Basically, it's all freehand airbrushing—filling in the stencil. Fill in light areas first, then airbrush in the darker areas. One trick I use to figure out if my airbrush is spraying correctly is to spray on the outline stencil next to where I want to spray, before I spray on the mural itself. This way, if the airbrush is not spraying perfectly, it won't ruin what I've done so far. I do this nearly every time I start airbrushing.

After the colors are roughed in, start refining them, getting some fur textures. **See fig. 9.** This can be done with hand-cut fur stencils: paper with jagged, tiny furry cuts along the edge. For the darker areas of the fur, I use tiny strokes with the airbrush in light tones, and then airbrush a wash of transparent black over it.

With a paper stencil, cut out the eye and place it over the eye. **See fig. 10.**

I use a round plastic drafting template for the eyeball. **See fig. 11.** Airbrush the eye with a white/yellow mix, layer a root beer color on, then softly airbrush the edges with very-reduced black. I make a black dot where the center of the iris will be, use that dot to center a smaller circle on the template, and then airbrush a black iris.

The tip of a very sharp, white Stabilo pencil is used for the highlight in the eye. **See fig. 12.**

Next, a paper stencil is used for the mouth. **See fig. 13.** I airbrush a red mix, softened by adding a bit of white and black, for the tongue. It gets its definition from details like the center ridge and the edges in black and pink.

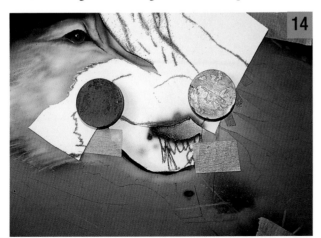

The gums are masked off and sprayed with black and red. **See fig. 14.** Then they are detailed with black and softly highlighted with pink, running the highlights along where the teeth stick into the gum.

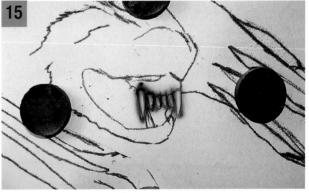

The teeth are cut out of a paper copy and airbrushed with white and black, and finely detailed with white. **See fig. 15.** Since I drew on the teeth, it is easy to line up the paper stencils.

109

OK, now I don't like the way this mural is going. **See fig. 16.** It doesn't have the dramatic effect I was trying for. I go through my reference bookcase and find two more wolf files with pictures I can use. I also pull two old files with notes on previous wolf murals I've done. There I find some ideas and fur-edge stencils I can use.

Now I tip the tank up, so I can more easily airbrush the muzzle wrinkles. (I airbrush better back and forth than up and down.) I completely rework the muzzle, starting by tracing on a new wrinkle design that comes directly from the reference photo. Then with light tones, I airbrush the new muzzle, highlighting the top of the wrinkles, then with the dark tones, airbrushing the deep, shadowed lines. All of this is done very, very softly. I'm relying on the Iwata Micron C, as I need very fine detail and very soft color variations.

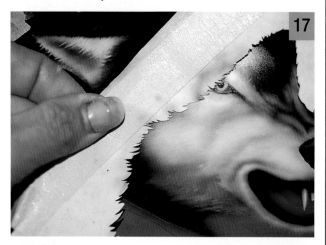

I hold up the fur-edge stencils, orienting them in the direction the fur runs, and softly spray light tones. **See figs. 17, 18, and 19.** Then I move the stencil a little, spray again, and keep repeating until either achieving a nice layout of fur or the desired results for the job. I also now notice that I have the teeth wrong, but shortening the right tooth easily changes it. I'm finally liking the face better, so I use a paper stencil and mask off the nose. The nose is sprayed with black. Highlights like the center ridge and tip of the nose are done with very reduced gray.

I use more paper stencils to define the nostrils: One is for the area between the nostrils, and one for the nostrils themselves. **See fig. 20.**

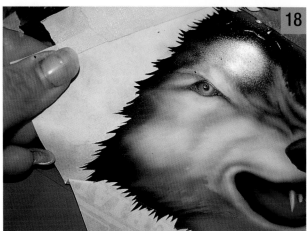

Now for the paws. I paper them off and spray them with very light tan. I use paper stencils to give hard edges to the toes. **See fig. 21.**

22

Shadow using dark tones, then freehand the shadows to soften the edges. **See fig. 22.** Highlight with the lighter tones, using the fur stencils, and shadow with black. I cut the toenails out of a paper copy that I use as a stencil. I spray them with black, then highlight with white.

23

I tip the tank up again and airbrush the shadows from the ripped bits over the paws. **See fig. 23.** Then I mask off the torn back part of the rip and shadow black along both edges.

24

I highlight along the center with white. You can get a three-dimensional edge to it by holding up the frisket cutout and spraying a little black.

The finished paw. **See fig. 24.**

25

The other paw is masked off and airbrushed. **See fig. 25.**

See how the soft tones eventually build up to form the highs and lows of the paw. Each toe is masked, and dark tones are sprayed behind it, creating shadows. Now the area behind the wolf is sprayed black, and the rips are taped

26

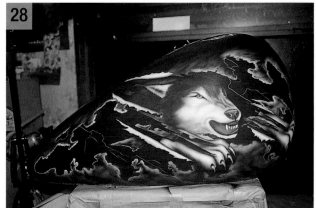

28

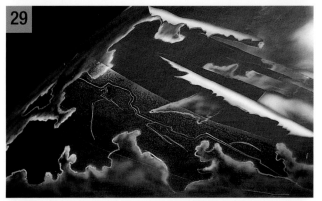

29

off and sprayed. **See fig. 26.** I use the cutout from the original stencil to edge the rips. I put the cutout near the edge, leaving a little gap, and spray soft black for the bottom rips and white for the top rips. I remove the frisket and wipe precleaner around the artwork, without touching it, to remove any adhesive.

I'm nearly done. Now it's ready for a round of clear. **See fig. 27.** I'll most likely refine the wolf a bit. The lightning will be added later, and I want to protect what I have so far.

The newly applied clear has dried overnight and has been wet sanded with 600 grit. It's time to add lightning. First, I draw the lightning on with a white Stabilo. **See fig. 28.**

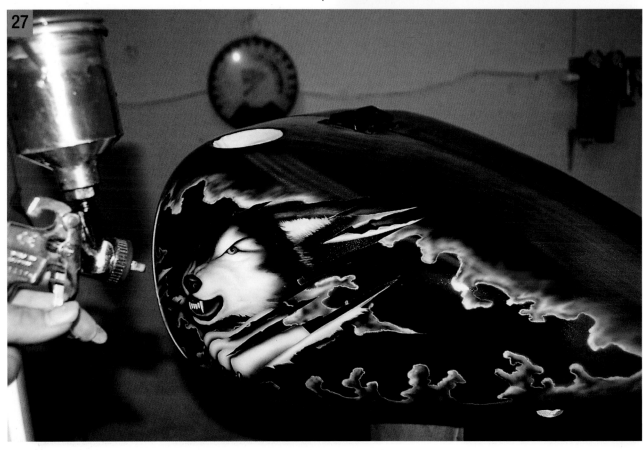

27

That area is then covered with frisket paper and the lightning bolt is cut out with a No. 4 stencil knife. **See fig. 29.** The rest of the tank is protected with masking paper. A thick white—not too thick—is airbrushed on. Don't do too many coats, or there'll be a thick paint edge. A good lightning bolt won't take much.

Now peel off the masking and frisket paper. **See fig. 30.** White overspray has a habit of sticking to places where frisket paper was applied, so carefully damp sand with 800 or 1,000 grit around the bolts, without running the sandpaper over them.

Using torn paper to mask off the cloud edge, and using a very reduced white base coat mix, I lightly airbrush the electric glow around each bolt. **See fig. 31.** If the white spray is grainy, add reducer.

Next I'm going to add a few more torn-back parts on the rips. I put frisket paper where I need the new tears to be, cut them out, and save the parts that are cut out. **See fig. 32.** Take care not to put the frisket over the newly applied lightning bolt paint.

Airbrush white down the center of the tear. **Fig. 33.**

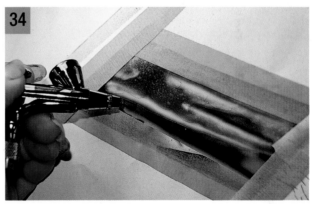

Airbrush very reduced black down the top and bottom. **See fig. 34.**

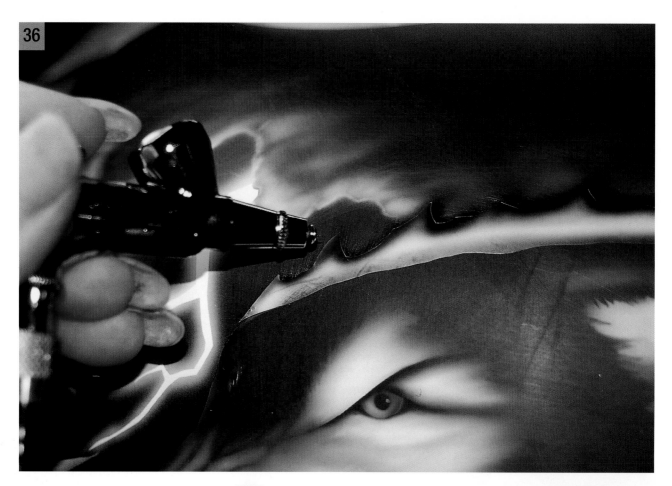

Use the cutouts to get a three-dimensional edge. Line them up along the edge leaving a gap, then spray a bit of black for bottom tears or white for upper tears. **See fig. 33.**

To get the shadow under the rip, lightly place the frisket cutout over the rip and spray black. **See fig. 34.** Just let the cutout "rest" on the rip; don't stick it on. Once I'm done, I'll give it four coats of clear urethane, making sure to go light on the first coat, since I don't want the uncleared artwork to run.

The finished product. **See fig. 35.**

A FEW WILDLIFE MURALS

38

This eagle is airbrushed mostly in silhouette. Some detail is visible, but the darkness of the artwork technique gives it a serious mood, very dramatic.

39

40

41

Large flowers and hummingbirds combine for simple but very effective murals. **See figs. 40 and 41.** The flowers are stenciled off, and one petal is sprayed at a time. And as you can see, that's pretty easy—just lights and darks and simple masking. The birds are one stencil, and then I use paper cutouts to get sharp details. These were fun murals to work on.

Another dramatic effect achieved using darkness. Only the face, talons, and few miscellaneous feathers are seen. The face and feet are stenciled off in frisket and airbrushed. Paper cut-out stencils are used for the details, then the stencils are removed and clear coat applied. After it is dry and sanded, the feather edges of the face are free-hand airbrushed with white, which covers over the hard stencil line and softens the effect.

The three zebras were also done with one single stencil with paper cut-outs for the sharp lines. Even the stripes were done with paper stencils.

Detail from jungle mural.

I had a great reference photo for this mural.

45 This evil dude fit perfectly here. I had the background webbing done and cleared already. A frisket paper stencil was used for the critter.

46

The neck of a softail. The gorilla seemed to be just the right fit. Again: great photo = great mural. It was fun, freehand airbrushing the background and the foreground grass.

CHAPTER 13
AIRBRUSHING EVIL SKULL FLAMES–THE FUN STUFF

MATERIAL AND EQUIPMENT

- Roll of transfer tape
- 1/16" 3M green Fine Line Tape
- Grafix frisket paper
- Masking tape
- Base coat paint colors for skull
- White
- Black
- Blue base tint
- Base coat clear or Intercoat clear
- Tracing paper (as transparent as you can find)
- Fine line permenant marker pens (these are found only in artist supply stores) such as
- Pigma Micron 005
- Sakura Microperm 01
- Koh-I-Noor Rapidograph
- Iwata HP-C airbrush
- Iwata Micron C airbrush
- Satagraph 2 airbrush
- Seamstress measuring tape (soft tape used in sewing)
- Small magnets
- Tweezers
- Light table or window
- Soft lead pencil
- Pink eraser
- X-acto No. 4 Knife
- X-acto No. 11 Knife

The first time I ever painted skull-head flames, the end result was pretty good. At least the skull part was—I still had a lot to learn about painting flames. I wish it had looked as good as the above photo.

Don't just rush into mural artwork. Do your research. When I started painting skulls, I looked at the work of airbrush artists I admired. I had a copy of *Gray's Anatomy* left over from art school that suddenly came in very handy. I looked at photos of skulls and took pictures of an actual human skull. I studied the way the light hits the bone and defines it. Go to a bookstore and buy books with good pictures of the subject matter you are painting. You will probably use them more than once—hopefully, you'll be

painting more of that subject in the future, so it's good to build up a reference library. Whenever possible, work from actual photographs and drawings of the subject matter. Slip a plastic sandwich bag over the photo to protect it from the paint overspray, and tape it close to where you're working. Sometimes I tape a photo right to the tank or part I am airbrushing.

Bone texture technique can vary widely. I have included a bunch of photos of skull and skull flame paint I have done to show the many different effects that you can obtain. Read through the step-by-step, and then plan out your design and process. Don't rush through it. Chances are you'll achieve even better results with your first skull flame paint than I did.

The first thing to do is evenly lay out the flames and skulls. **See fig. 2.** I start with the right side of an H-D Softail tank and a skull template. It's easy to make one. I have gathered an extensive reference library of skull pictures over the years. They're not hard to find.

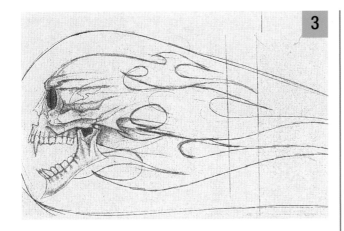

Here is the skull I drew for this paint. **See fig. 3.** If you can't just draw a skull, then go online or to a bookstore and look up skull photos or drawings. Anatomy books, like *Gray's Anatomy*, can be a big help.

Draw out the skull you want and make a copy of it. Don't mess with your original. Refer to Chapter 5 for details. Now take some frisket paper and make a stencil of the skull. **See fig. 4.**

Use a light table to trace the stencil. **See fig. 5.** If you don't have a light table, during daylight hours, tape the template to a window, then tape some frisket paper over it and trace away. Now flip the template over and trace the skull again on another piece of frisket paper. This will be used on the opposite side. OK, now you have the skulls for both sides of the tank ready. I use Grafix frisket film (paper). It's matte finish, so it's easy to draw on and low tack. Frisket papers are not all alike. Some use a cheap adhesive that leaves residue.

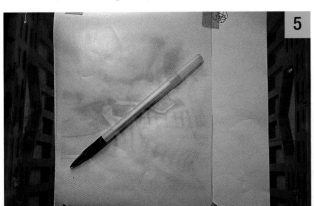

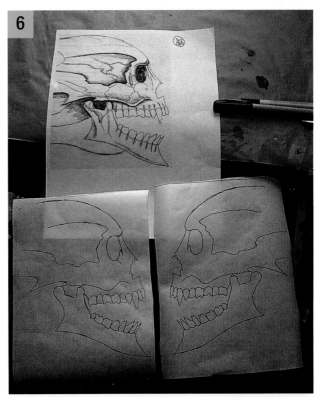

Using a No. 4 X-acto knife, cut out the skulls. **See fig. 6.** I use a drawing board with a thin piece of cardboard on it for a cutting surface. See Chapter 5 for more details.

Next, place the skull template or cutout where you want it at the front of the tank, then lay out the flames behind it. **See fig. 7.** Refer to Chapter 6 as you go through the flame-painting process.

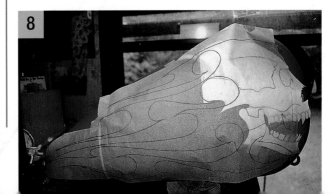

Sometimes, I do my flame layout figuring on tracing paper. For this project, I chose to do that rather than freehand layout the flame design with tape. Here I taped a piece of tracing paper down and drew the flames on that. **See fig. 8.**

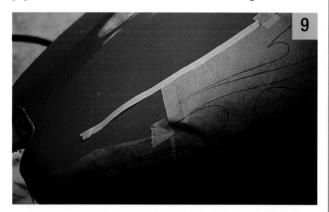

Make sure to put tape along the edges of the tracing paper and draw lines that run from the paper to the marking tape. **See fig. 9.** This trick can help you replace the tracing paper in the exact same position.

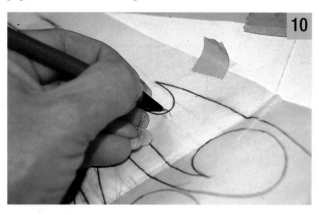

Remove the tracing paper, flip it over, and using a lead pencil, trace along the flame outline. **See fig. 10.** Next, return the tracing paper outline to the tank, using the tape and marks as a guide.

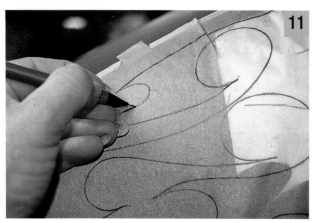

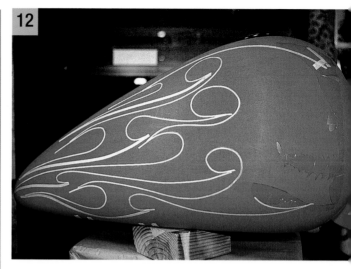

Trace along the flame outline, which leaves a nice neat flame design in pencil on the tank surface. **See fig. 11.**

Using 1/16-inch green fine line tape, tape off the flames. **See fig. 12.** Secure the curves of the flame with a bit of tape. Using the templates as a guide, place your skull stencils around the template.

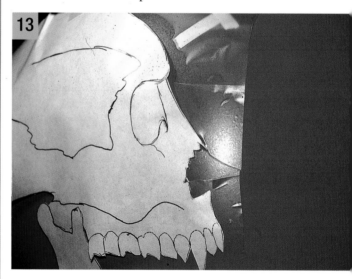

You're going to have to cut the stencil into pieces, because the stencil is flat and the tank is round. **See fig. 13.** Use common sense to decide the exact layout of the skull outline stencil. Tape up any spaces, and use tape to carefully even up any areas where the edges of the stencil don't line up perfectly. When that's complete, remove the template. Now cut out a piece of tracing paper that will cover both the flames and the skull. Tape it over them and use a soft lead pencil to trace the entire outline. This will be used to line up the design on the other side of the tank.

You'll need to pick a few places to use as points of reference. **See fig. 14.** I like to use the following places: from the nose of the skull to the front edge of the tank, from the top

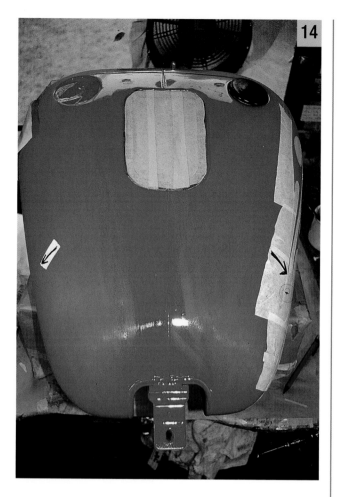

14

Now tape off the flames and skulls, using transfer tape and masking tape (refer to Chapter 6 for details). **See fig. 15.** Be sure to remove any lead pencil markings from the flame surface—use a pink eraser and carefully rub those lines away. Then, using a dry airbrush with the pressure turned up, blow away any debris left from the eraser.

In cases such as this one where the flames are white, there is no need to tape off the skull. In other styles of skull flames, like thick-coated candy or dark pearl flames, you may want to tape off the skull. Pick a point where you want the flames to blend into the skull, then tape off the skull. Now spray those flames. In this example, I did a three-color pearl fade: HOK Snow White Pearl to HOK Silver Pearl to HOK Platinum Pearl.

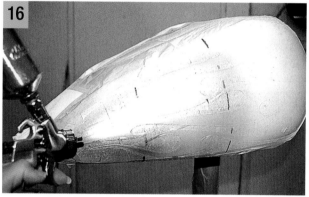

16

I marked the flame area into three separate sections (as a fade guide) before I sprayed the flames. **See fig. 16.** I then used a few light coats of DBC 500 base coat clear over the pearl flames. You can also use House of Kolor Intercoat Clear SG-100.

17

of the skull to the middle seam on top of the tank, from various flame points to the top seam of the tank, and a rough bottom measurement like from the bottom of the flames to the bottom edge of the tank. Using a soft measuring tape, take these measurements and lay out the same points on the opposite side of the tank. Next, place the tracing-paper stencil on that side, using the tape layout points to know where to place it. Once the tracing paper is taped on securely, take a pencil and carefully trace the flames and skull. Now both sides will have a good chance of matching. Using the pencil outline as a guide, place the other skull stencil outline on that side and then lay out your flames with 1/16-inch green fine line tape.

While the paint dries, take the skull template, flip it over, place it on a light table or against a window, and trace the reverse side. **See fig. 17.** Now make six or seven copies of both sides on a scanner/printer or copy machine. Then cut out things like eyes, jaws, cheekbones, and such using a No. 11 X-acto Knife. You'll be using these cutouts as specialized

15

stencils to get sharp detail around the eye sockets, nasal cavity, teeth, and cheekbones—anywhere you want a hard edge.

Once the flame paint is dry, remove any paper that was taped over the skulls. Softly and carefully sand any edge that formed. Don't sand too far up the flame. Then, just past that line, tape off the flames from the skulls, so overspray from the skulls doesn't wander onto the flames. You'll blend the skulls into the flames later. If you sprayed the skull area when you sprayed the flames, carefully and lightly sand the skull area with 1,000 grit.

Now you can mix up your skull colors. I do cool-color skulls using white, black, and blue/black mixtures. I mix the colors thinned down about one part color to two parts reducer, using PPG DBC base colors, and DMD 1684 for black. For the blue and black mix, I take some of the reduced 1684 and add some DMD 660 blue toner. I use either DT 885 or DT 898 (for very fine detail work) for reducer. I put these color mixes into bottles, then pour off a little bit into another bottle and thin it down even more, leaving six bottles with color. Sometimes I will use three differently reduced bottles of the same color: one color to get good coverage, one use for gradual shading, and one to use for very light shading or fine detail work. Use your own judgment and experience to determine what works best for you.

Next take some of the thicker white and airbrush it over the surface of the skull.

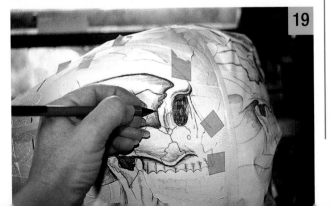

While the white is drying, take one of the copies of the template, flip it over onto a light box or window, and using a soft pencil, trace the main features and lines of the skull: the eye sockets, cheekbones, and other details. **See fig. 18.**

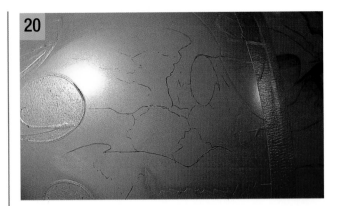

Now place it over the skull stencil layout and trace along the lines you want to transfer to the surface of the tank. You're basically copying the skull design onto the tank. **See fig. 19.**

Any soft or blurry lines can now be drawn onto the skull surface with a pencil. **See fig. 20.**

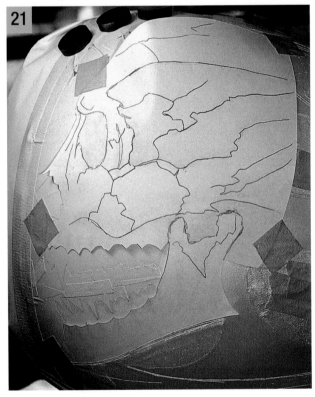

For the opposite side of the tank just flip the stencil over. **See fig. 21.**

122

23

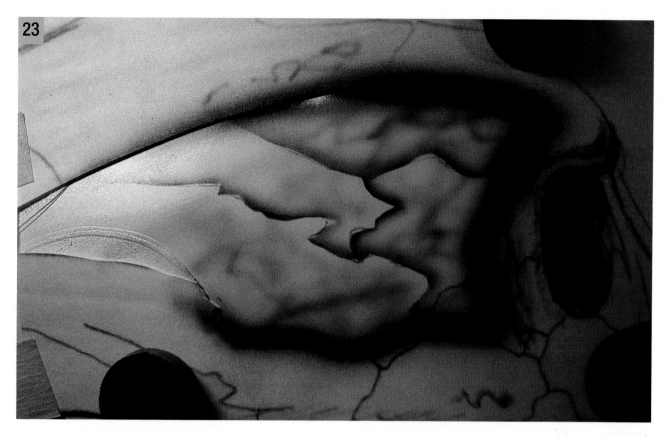

Now you can start airbrushing. **See fig. 22.** I usually start at the top of the skull, get that area done, then proceed to the eyebrows, eyes, and work my way down.

One neat trick involves taking one of the skull template copies and drawing cracks on it. Make a few copies of that. Then cut along the cracks and use those to make cracks in the bone surface. Put down the top half of the paper and lightly spray black, then blue/black, then put down the lower half of the paper and lightly spray white. This is done because of the way the light hits a crack, the bottom part is in shadow, and the top part catches light. Now take a black art pen and softly draw on the crack itself. To secure the stencil cutouts and crack lines, I use small round magnets and pieces of tape. The magnet will make marks on the paint, especially the white, so

don't let the magnet touch the mural painted surface, only place it on the paper. For the bits of tape, I take 3/4-inch tape and cut off a bunch of half-inch pieces and line them up on a nearby surface for quick access.

To build up the bone texture, start with the blue/black mixture and airbrush it where you think the hollows and cracks of the skull would be. **See fig. 23.**

Then take the white and softly start to build up the high points of the bone surface. **See fig. 24.** Once the white is on, go over the dark cracks or depressions with both of the darker mixtures, sharpening up the detail. Now, do a bit more sharpening up with the white. After that, pull the airbrush away and apply a soft white fade to soften up the whole surface, letting the highlights glow with the white.

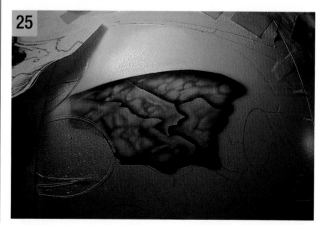

24

25

26

Just work your way around the skull. **See fig. 25.**

As you go, it will get easier. You'll start to see the cracks. **See fig. 26.** You don't actually want to have the skull surface covered with defined cracks; your goal is to give the impressions of cracks, like the surface of marble.

27

For the eye-socket area, use the cutout copies to lay out the high and low points of the eye socket. **See fig. 27.**

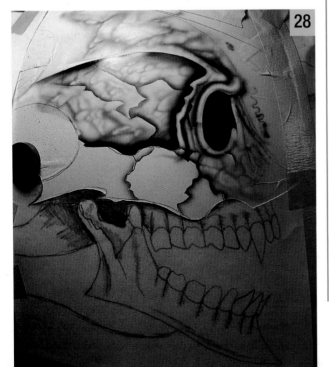
28

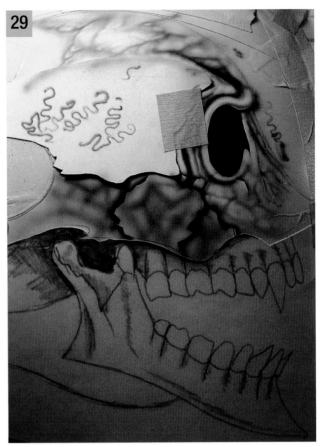
29

The surface of the skull is formed by the combined use of freehand techniques and cutouts. Here I used one of the crack cutouts and airbrushed with black. **See fig. 28.**

Mask off a section and freehand the detail, maybe even drawing the line detail lightly with a pencil, then airbrushing along it. **See fig. 29.** Here I freehanded blue/black over the cracks.

You can see that I started airbrushing in the white highlights on the finished cheekbone. **See fig. 30.** I softly airbrushed a white highlight line so the light would catch the top of the bone. I also added a shadow toward the bottom of the bone. This gives it the three-dimensional effect.

A word of advice: Don't expect to get great results in the first five minutes. It takes time to really get the end product you want, and it needs to build up gradually. Be patient. It may take a few hours of playing around with your technique before you finally start to see the bone surface give the three-dimensional illusion. Little by little, the mural will take shape and you'll begin to feel more comfortable. That's when it will start coming together. For early areas that have substandard results, just go back over them. That's one of the great things about working on murals: You can always go back and rework areas until you're happy with them. Never rush it or push yourself the first time you try something new. Give yourself plenty of time, work little by little, and try not to turn it into a torture session.

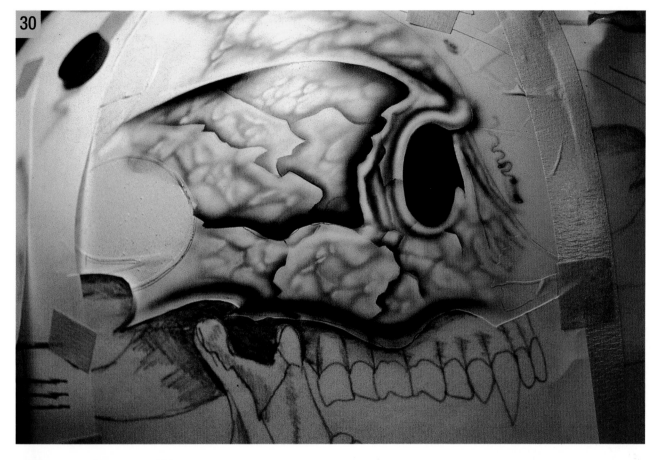

30

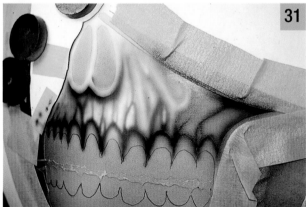

31

low I keep the pressure, it's just something that happens. I usually go back over my black areas (like the eyes) with black, and the dark areas (like the eye sockets) with a light wash of the black/blue. This sharpens up and further defines those areas.

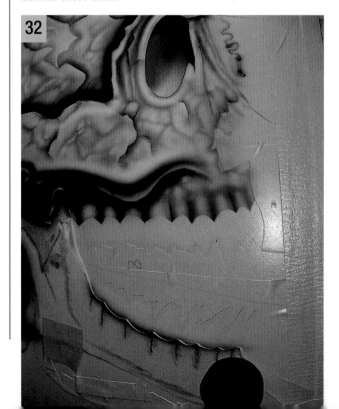

32

This photo, from a different paint job, aptly demonstrates the effectiveness of playing around with highlights and shadowing. **See fig. 31.** The surface comes to life as white is added. Experiment as you go, explore ideas, and find your own technique to get the kind of surface you want. This example uses cool colors, but skulls can also be done with warm colors. Mixtures of brown, yellow, and red, along with the black and white, give you a more realistic skull. I have a few actual animal skulls in my shop, and they are more brown and cream than white. But my style tends toward a whiter skull.

During this process, the white tends to make a slight overspray that travels onto the black areas. No matter how

125

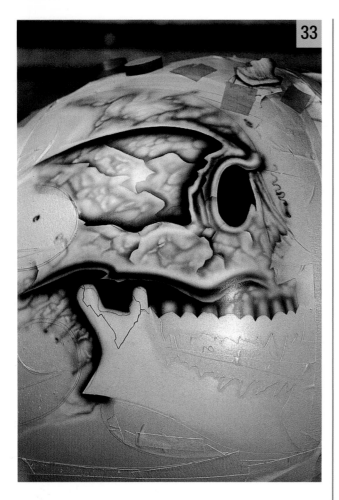

I've started airbrushing the mouth area, using the same techniques. **See fig. 32.**

Starting on the jawbone with drawn-on cracks. **See fig. 33.**

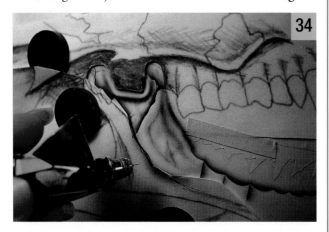

After using the crack stencils to shadow the cracks, I freehand the dark cracks and hollows in the bone. **See fig. 34.**

Freehanding the white highlights, the bottom half is done, and the top part is ready for white highlights. **See fig. 35.** Note how everything but the jaw is papered off with the stencils cut out previously.

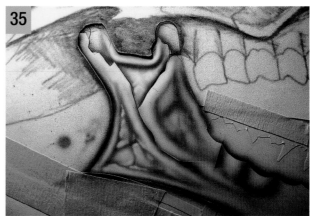

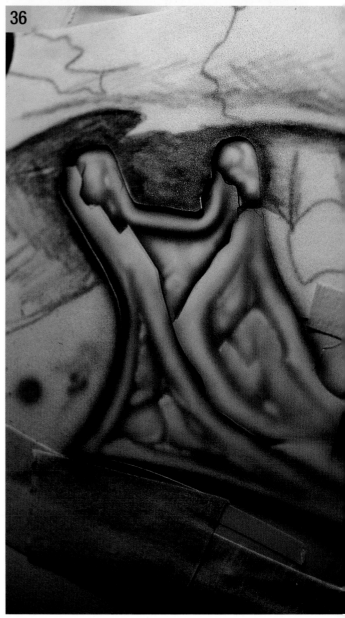

Nearly done! **See fig. 36.**

126

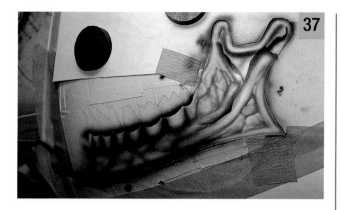

Working my way down to the teeth area, freehanding black tint. **See fig. 37.**

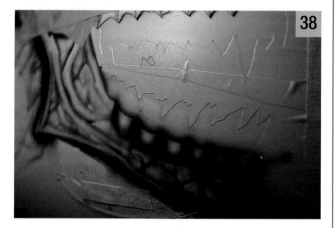

Freehand airbrushing white. I'm now ready to do the teeth. **See fig. 38.**

For airbrushing the skull teeth, I have two methods. The method pictured here is to mask off the line of teeth with a paper stencil. Then take a slightly curved paper, tape it on, and airbrush the edge of a tooth. I go right down the line of teeth. **See fig. 39.**

Then I go back and freehand in the white highlights, soften them with a bit of blue/black mix, then hit them again with a bit of white. **See fig. 40.**

The other method uses the stencil copies: I cut out a few teeth from each of the copies. I then spray each tooth individually, lining up the tooth cutouts with the pencil line reference I drew on before I started airbrushing. As the teeth are airbrushed, give a few of them cracks, or even shadowy hints of cracks. Don't overdo it; just a little bit will give the maximum effect.

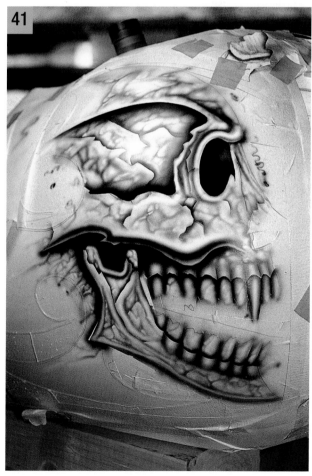

Once the skull is complete, carefully pull off the tape and paper covering the flames. **See fig. 41.** Using the black, start to blend the skull into the flames at the taped-off points. Then use the black, white, and blue/black. Don't carry the blend back too far, just far enough to make a gradual fade.

Next, peel away the transfer tape, frisket paper, and fine line tape, in that order. Carefully remove any loose paint edge that sticks up by softly rubbing or carefully cutting with the No. 4 knife or razor. Precleaner should be wiped around artwork without touching it to remove any frisket adhesive. Next, using 1,000-grit paper, very carefully wet sand around the skull and flames, removing any paint that had strayed beyond the tape and stencils. Sometimes there are also marks that mysteriously appear. Wet sanding removes any surprises that might show up after clear coat. Take care not to touch the flames or the skulls with the sandpaper.

Note that I did not apply any kind of clear or Intercoat Clear over the skulls. Since very thinned down white base coat was used on the skulls, clearing over them with base coat clear might mute or wash out those tones. Next, wash down the surface with a wet cloth to remove any leftover loose paint edge and bits from those paint edges. After wiping off the tank and making certain the surface is clean, apply urethane clear coat. The trick here is to spray the first two coats on very lightly. They aren't even full coats. Once those coats have set up, spray a few medium coats, then a few heavy coats. The next day, wet sand the clear with 600 grit, but don't sand too much, and don't sand through the edges of the skulls or flames.

Next, do any rework to the skulls you want and repeat the clearing process. Don't be afraid to do rework. Every airbrush artist usually sees something he or she wants to rework. If you aren't happy with your rework, simply wet sand it off and try again. Your base artwork is fine, because it is buried under clear. You're free to retouch and rework until your skull is as evil and sharply defined as you want it to be.

If you run into any problems with the flames, refer to Chapters 6 and 7.

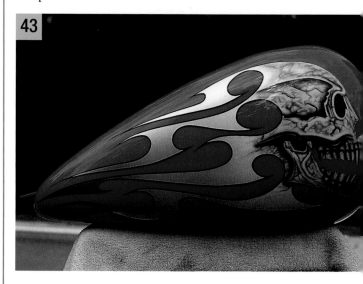

43

42

The finished results! **See figs. 42 and 43.** These techniques can be used to airbrush any kind of skull at any angle. I used the same technique, with slight variations, in all the skull paint photos seen here. Keep in mind that the better a picture or drawing you have to work from, the more realistic the skull will look.

44

45

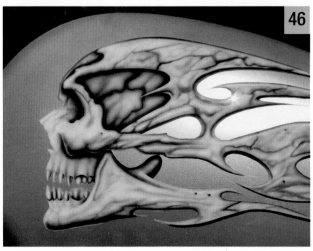

46

47

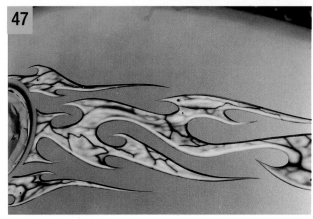

You can also use this skull painting method to paint bones, as seen in figure 44. To get the proper perspective for this mural on an airdam, I took a photo of my hand on the airdam in the position I wanted the skeleton hand.

I used House of Kolor Kandy Koncentrates: Oriental Blue KK-04 and Purple KK-10 mixed with HOK Intercoat Clear SG-100 to shade this skull, helping it to accent the flame color. **See fig. 45.**

In this paint job, I carried the bone effect across the entire flame surface. **See fig. 46.**

In this close-up photo of bone-effect flames, you can see how the bone airbrushing technique can really bring the surface to life. **See fig. 47.** Here I placed 1/8-inch green fine line tape along the edges, laid 1/16-inch tape alongside it and then taped off one side with 3/4-inch masking tape. Then I removed the 1/8-inch tape and sprayed along the edge, creating a shadow. I did this before I removed the material masking off the flames themselves.

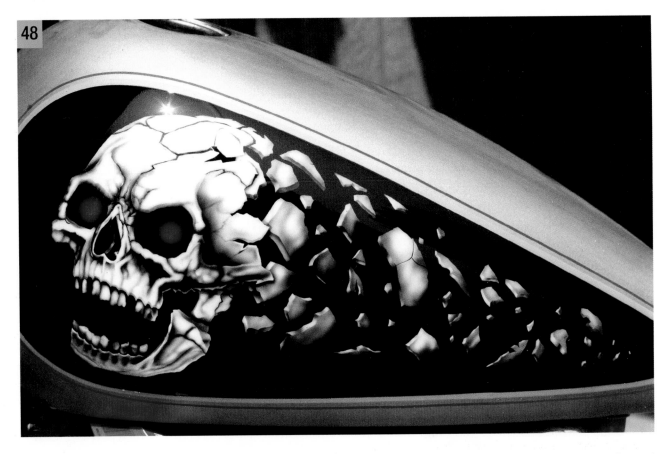

48

The rest of the photos just show the different kinds of skulls, with and without flames, that I have created using these methods.

Here I broke up the back of the skull and let the pieces flow across the tank. **See fig. 48.**

Sunglasses give a whole new twisted effect to a forward facing skull. **See fig. 49.** For the sunglasses, simply lay a pair of sunglasses on a computer scanner or copier bed and make a copy to use a stencil reference.

49

50

Or you can add a hat. For this, I took a photo of myself with a hat on to use as a reference. **See fig. 50.** (The skull face, of course, isn't mine. It came from another photo!)

All kinds of skull effects are seen here, including sneaky guys peeking in from behind the graphic, which are simply shaded with black. **See fig. 51.**

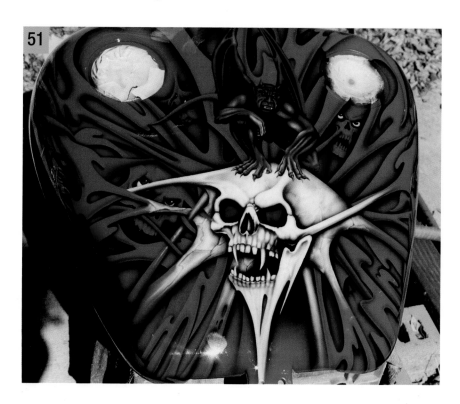

51

CHAPTER 14
PAINTING A PINUP GIRL

MATERIAL AND EQUIPMENT

- Grafix Frisket Paper
- Avery Yellow Paint Mask #A1830-S
- Transfer Tape
- Stabilo Pencils
- Lead pencil
- Base coat colors
- White
- Gray
- Black
- Dark brown mixture
- "Root beer" transparent toner
- Red
- Yellow
- Iwata HP-C airbrush
- Iwata Micron C airbrush
- Satagraph 2 airbrush
- X-acto No. 4 Stencil Knife (for frisket)
- X-acto No.11 Knife (for paper)
- Uncle Bill's Sliver Grippers
- Light table or window
- Magnets

1

2

Airbrushing pinup girls, portraits, and characters is not as complex as it may seem. A simple system of stencils and tape-offs can help it go smoothly and quickly.

It was quite a treat to reproduce an actual 1950s pinup girl for this step-by-step. **See fig. 2.** Sun Drop Beverages provided me with a copy of the original art. They wanted to celebrate their 50th anniversary by giving away a new 2004 Harley-Davidson Sportster.

First I wiped the new stock tank with precleaner several times until the surface squeaked when I rubbed it. Next the tank was wet sanded with 600 grit. Be careful not to sand through the clear coat, which can be kind of thin on factory paint jobs.

I made copies of the artwork in various sizes and tried them on the tank, letting the customer pick the one he thought fit best for his purposes. I had to do a little redrawing around the hidden leg and foot, because the bottle was left out of the mural. Once that was done, I slapped the artwork on a light table, put a piece of frisket paper over it, and traced it, creating a stencil. Making copies of the traced stencil and original artwork is the next step. Make about five of each.

Cut out the stencil with a No. 4 stencil knife. With magnets or tape, attach the cutout to the tank, lining it up. Now stick the stencil around the cutout, cutting it apart every few inches, as the tank is round and the stencil is flat. **See fig. 3.** This way, you avoid folds in the stencil and it will lie flat. I took the stencil cutout and ran off a few copies on the computer. They can be seen to the left of the tank.

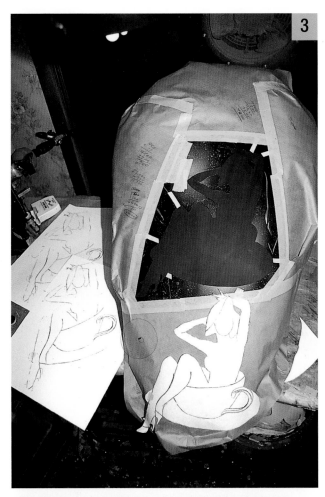

3

I started with the coffee cup. I cut out the girl from one of the copies and stuck her in place on the tank, using magnets and tape. **See fig. 4.** That way, I was only painting the cup-and-saucer part of the mural. There wouldn't be any paint edges that cut through the girl. If she were not masked off, those edges would be a problem.

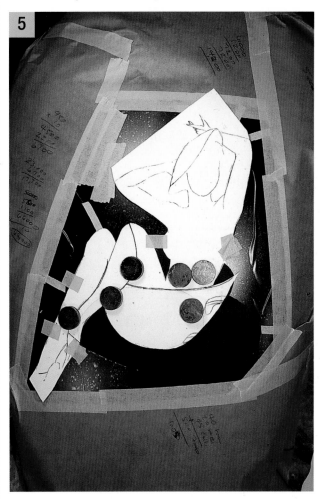

5

Next, the cup and saucer were cut out. The cup was put into place, and the saucer airbrushed, using white, gray, and very-reduced black. **See fig. 5.** It wasn't easy to reference such old and worn-looking artwork, especially for the cup and saucer. I had to imagine where the highs and lows were. I found a similar cup and saucer in my kitchen and posed them at the same light angle for a better reference.

First, the whole saucer is sprayed with gray.

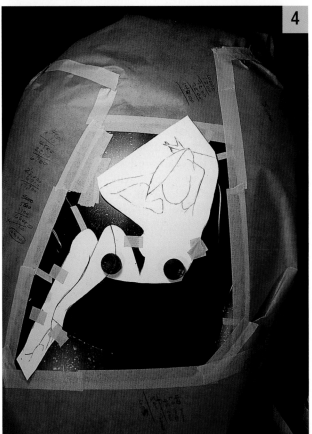

4

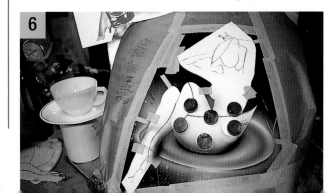

6

133

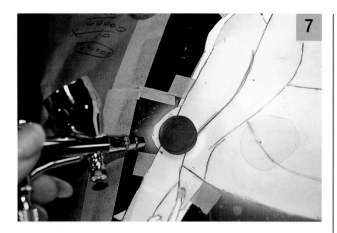

7

10

The raised areas are softly airbrushed with very-reduced white base coat, and the low points are softly sprayed with very-reduced black. **See fig. 6.**

To get the edge of the saucer, place the cutout saucer 1/8 inch from the edge of the stencil and lightly spray white. **See fig. 7.**

The inner part of the cup is masked off, and that area is quickly airbrushed. **See fig. 9.**

Now for the handle. Cut out the handle from one of the copies and use that for the stencil. **See fig. 10.**

8

Now the cup is masked off from the saucer and girl. **See fig. 8.** The handle will be added later. Repeat the method used with the saucer. The whole cup is sprayed with gray. Black is shadowed around the bottom. The rim is detailed by using cut out stencils and spraying white to define the edge.

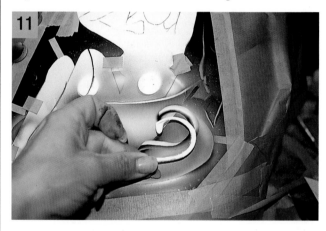

11

The highlights and shadows on the handle that give it the three-dimensional look are obtained by cutting out those areas on a copy of the stencil cutout. **See fig. 11.** Once those are softly airbrushed in, remove the stencil, and lightly go over the edges with very-reduced white and black. Places where white has crept past the stencil are redefined with black. I keep all the stencils I have been making very handy. I tape them in a line on my light box or a crate right next to my chair.

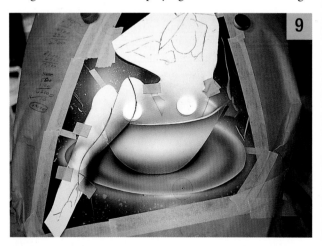

9

12

PAINTING A PINUP GIRL

13

I tape off the cup and saucer. **See fig. 12.** I'm ready to start airbrushing the body. I'll start with the legs.

I've heard other artists complain that airbrushing skin tones can be a pain. I used to think so too, but I've found a quick and easy way to mix skin tones, using only a few colors, that never has that muddy look.

I always use base coat enamels and their toners. Whatever paint system you are using, make sure you know all the tints available. Most paint systems have a brownish, almost root-beer-colored tint that is transparent. PPG's DMD tint number for this color is 623. Mix a little of this with white, maybe a little yellow, add a drop of red, and you'll have skin-tone color. Here I'm using my skin-tone mixture: a mix of skin tone lightened up with white, the root beer toner I spoke of, a mix of brown base coat/root beer/black,

and black. **See fig. 13.** I usually continue to mix more shades of skin tone as I progress through the mural. By the time I'm done, I'll have seven colors: black, root beer/brown/black mix, dark skin tone (darkened with the root beer tint), regular skin tone, light skin tone, very-light skin tone, and white. I also have two bottles of each color, one thicker for coloring in, and one really thinned down for soft, gradual shading. Exactly how much to thin the colors is something you'll have to play around with, as each brand of paint is different. Basically, try to keep thinning it down until the paint airbrushes on finely, but not grainy. I find that I achieve the best skin tones by layering on transparent tones of color. The healthy skin glow is the underpainted skin tones illuminating up through the top layers.

15

14

The right leg is taped off. **See fig. 14.**

Start out by airbrushing the skin tone along the high point of the leg. **See fig. 15.** The sides of the leg will be darker, so concentrate the spray in the middle, but spray a little bit on the upper calf. I have taped the original art right above the mural so I have a quick reference.

Next, mask off from the knee down with a paper stencil. **See fig. 16.** The root beer tint is airbrushed along the edges; I spray exactly where I see the shadows on the original photo. Follow that by softly spraying some brown mix along those edges, but don't bring it out as far as the root beer tint. With each darker color, less area is sprayed as the lighter color before. Now remove the mask, mask off the upper leg, and start airbrushing the darker tones. The left leg will drape over the right one, so use the black, and lightly spray a black shadow. The trick to getting the skin tones perfect is going very softly with the various colors—it's always better to use too little than too much. Keep the fades, highlights, and shadows very soft.

To keep the leg in the proper perspective and form, airbrush as if it were a whole leg, not a leg that is partially hidden. Then spray the shadow. You don't want the leg to curve around the area in which the other leg covers it.

Add a very soft shadow with the root beer-and-brown mix to define the calf. **See fig. 17.** Make a small paper cutout for the ankle, hold up the top half, and then spray dark shadow colors. Then hold up the bottom half and spray a small bit of skin tone; very lightly go over it free-hand to soften up the line. Now go back over the light areas with just a hint of the lighter skin tone and add just a hint of white in the center of that lighter area. Then go softly over the shadows with the root beer.

Let it dry a bit. In some murals I would go to another area not directly connected to the legs and work on that, but that is not the case here. I take a break.

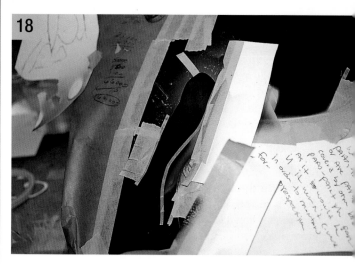

A half hour later, or when the paint is dry enough for tape not to leave a mark, mask off the right leg with fine line and masking tape. **See fig. 18.** The left leg was not visible in the original art, so I had to imagine it. Simply repeat the process used with the right leg, then draw out the ankle detail on paper, cut out the outline, and use that for a stencil. Put up the top half and spray dark tone.

Put up the bottom half and spray some light tone, then fade in dark tone below it, shadowing it. **See fig. 19.** Airbrush skin tone where the high points are and softly fade

in the shadows, using a progression of darkening shades. Go over the light areas with the lighter skin tones, add a soft highlight with white, and then lightly go over the shadows with root beer and/or the brown mix. Maybe even lightly go over the black. Small items, like getting good detail on things like ankles and knees, can make all the difference in how successfully a mural like this turns out. The process is fairly simple, once you get used to it.

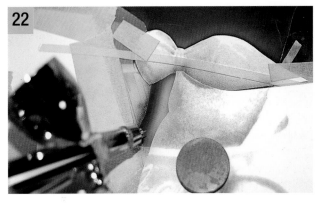

It's time to mask off the upper half of the girl. **See fig. 20.** A paper cutout covers the bikini and face. Make sure the bottom half of the mural is well taped and papered off. It would be no fun to have spilled paint ruining all the work you've done so far.

Repeat the same skin tone process on the upper half. Here, the paper stencil cutouts made from the copies come in very handy in placing the tummy or ab definitions in the right place. **See fig. 21.**

Use one half to get a sharp edge on the lighter side. **See fig. 22.** Line up the cutout, spray light skin tone, then remove that and put on the other half for definition on the other side, softly spraying darker tones. Again, refer to the original to see where to airbrush lights and darks.

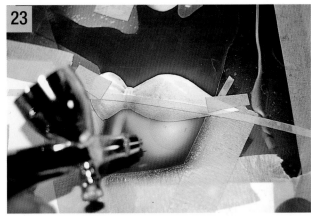

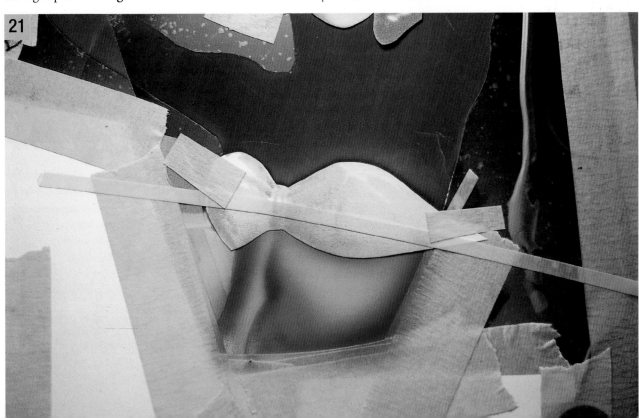

24

Softly spray very-reduced white to highlight the rib cage. **See fig. 23.**

Now for the upper body. **See fig. 24.** The tummy is protected by thick masking paper. Start by airbrushing skin tone on the high points.

25

Use paper stencil cutouts to get sharp detail on various areas you desire it. **See fig. 25.** I use them on the chest. You can already see the body coming to life. Try to sketch out most of the body with skin tone before shading in the darker tones.

26

Here the root beer tint and brown mix is softly shaded in. **See fig. 26.** The sharp detail on the chest is obtained by

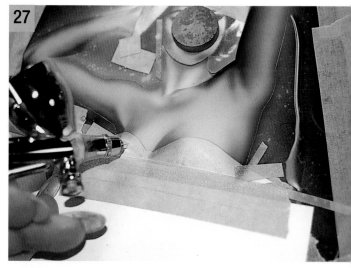

27

using the other half of the paper cutout used in the previous step. Any place there's a sharp line in the photo or art you are using, make a cutout of it.

Little by little, fade in the darker tones and shadows freehand. **See fig. 27.** As you airbrush along cutouts, the body will form. When you spray dark tone, complement it with darker tone. When you spray light, highlight it with lighter tone.

28

The white highlights, while very, very slight, add a great deal of dimension. **See fig. 28.**

29

30

Wow, she's almost done. **See fig. 29.** You can really see how all that soft shading added up, without having used much black. I used very thin, transparent black, although it is much darker where the legs crossed.

The area around the face and hair is masked off with fineline tape and paper stencils. **See fig. 30.** Use the hat cutout to help get the face into proper position.

I also cut out a hair stencil to get the hairline.

Spray the face with skin tone. Make a paper cutout of the face, flip it over, place it on a light table or window, and finely trace the details like eyes and lips. This is the back side of the cutout. **See fig. 31.**

Now flip it back over, line it up on the face, and carefully trace the eyes, nose and mouth. **See fig. 32.** Use a mechanical pencil with the tip sharpened to get the lines very fine. (Sharpen the tip by holding the pencil at angle and rub it back and forth while rolling it.)

31

32

33

The various brown tones are now airbrushed around the edges of the face and beneath the hairline. **See fig. 34.** Lightly airbrush the cheeks with root beer toner, then a little brown mix. Use Stabilo pencils to outline the eyes and softly draw in the eyelashes. Lightly spray the eyebrows with the brown mix using a paper stencil.

Now for the mouth—place a paper stencil over it and spray a mix of red tinted with a little brown and black.

35

Here you can see the traced-on face. Make a bunch of face-detail cutouts, one with the eyes cut out, one with the mouth cut out, etc. Here the nose cutout is placed on the face and root beer toner is sprayed. **See fig. 33.**

Reduce down the colors used on the face as much as you can. The finest detail will be needed here. If the paint is the least bit grainy, thin it down a little more; you need the brushes to spray an extremely fine line. For jobs like this, all the crown caps on the very end of gravity feed airbrushes should be removed. If you do this, be careful not to drop an airbrush, as the expensive needle and tip will be ruined without the protection of the crown cap.

34

See fig. 35. Spray pink along the edge of a paper stencil for the lower lip highlight. Also spray black along a stencil edge to define the bottom of the upper lip.

White was sprayed on a stencil for the teeth, and the mouth was done. See fig. 36.

After lining up an eye stencil, spray white over the eyes. See fig. 37. I make dots with a pencil to show me where to

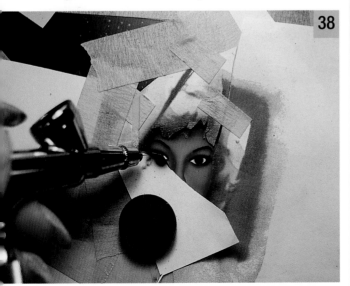

line up the eyeball stencil, and then I use a cut out to spray black on them. Use a plastic drafting template with various-sized circles. Just pick the circle with the size you want.

The ankle stencil can come in very handy on the face. Spray black along its edge—defining the eyes and lashes. See fig. 38. Move the stencil a bit, spray, move it, spray more, and so on.

Now airbrush some lighter skin tones and bring this face to life. See fig. 39. Line up the mouth cutout and lightly—very lightly—spray light skin tone around the mouth.

The finished face. See fig. 40. You can see how all those paper cutouts really came in handy. I used them above and below the eyebrows and sprayed lighter tones. I also (extremely softly) airbrushed light skin tone, then a bit of white along the line of the nose, the cheeks, the chin, and forehead. Again using paper stencils, I removed the tape around the face and masked off the hair using the face cutout, using white and black to airbrush the hair. I used my Iwata Custom Micron C to get the very fine lines of the hair.

Fine line tape is used to tape off the lower portion of the hair before it's airbrushed. See fig. 41.

41

42

Next the hat area is masked off and painted with white and black using fine line tape to get the black border. **See fig. 42.**

Nearly done! All that's left is the bikini top and shoes. **See fig. 43.**

Tape off the bikini top with fine line, trim with a No. 4 stencil knife, and then mask off. **See fig. 44.**

Use the same technique to mask off the shoes. The bikini and shoes will be painted at the same time. **See fig. 45.**

Use yellow, root beer tone, white, and the brown mix. **See fig. 46.** Freehand airbrush the entire bikini and shoes, with the exception of the center trim of the top. For that, quickly tape off with fine line, and then airbrush it. Use back and forth strokes. Any sharp edges are airbrushed against a tape edge. Remove the frisket and wipe precleaner around the artwork, without touching it, to remove any adhesive. So far, so good. Go to Chapter 15 for clear coat information.

Four coats of uro clear were applied and dried overnight. Once the clear is wet sanded, it's time for rework—I don't like the white hair, and my customer agrees. I mask off the hair again, using a combination of frisket and fine line tape. **See fig. 47.** She is transformed into a blonde by layering an airbrushed yellow/white/root beer tone mixture streaked with brown and highlighted with white. White highlights are added to the eyes using a white Stabilo pencil, which has a very sharp point on it. A darker shadow is added under the jaw.

We're finally happy with the pinup girl, and now all that's left is to put the vintage logo on the coffee cup. I waited until after the clear coat, because if I didn't like the way it looked, I could damp sand it off without bothering the artwork below it. The logo stencil is hand-cut from Avery Yellow Paint Mask. **See fig. 48.** Place transfer tape over the stencil before peeling the backing off.

48

50

Use a paper cutout of the cup and place it against the stencil. **See fig. 49.** Use a light box or window to line up the lettering. Then cut around the cup to transfer the cup shape to the stencil.

Peel the backing off and line the stencil up, then stick it in place. **See fig. 50.** Spray on brown first, then lightly airbrush yellow along the center of the lettering. Now you're ready for the second round of clear.

49

51

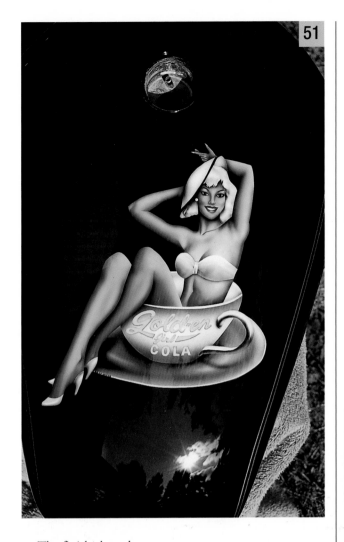

The finished product.

52

This very involved mural took a lot of predrawing and planning. See figs. 52, 53, and 54. I had a handsome guy pose for the photo that I used for the angel. For the reaper, I took a photo of myself in a robe posed in the same position as the reaper. That way I had a perfect reference for airbrushing the folds of the robe.

53

54

CHAPTER 15
THE GREAT CLEAR COAT DEBATE

No single issue in custom painting is as hotly debated as clear coating. Some painters insist that the only way to seal artwork is to use base coat clear, sometimes with hardener added. Other painters swear by urethane clears. As for filler clear, the same argument rages on, with one camp on the base coat side, the other on the uro side. Shop conditions, equipment, and weather generally determine what's possible, but only the painter can know what truly works best for him or her. My best advice is to use the clear coat method with which you are most comfortable.

Base coat clears can be the way to go. They're less expensive than uro clear, and in some cases they dry harder and faster. If a painter is on a tight budget, base coat clear is worth considering. I do my filler clear with urethane clear, because that's the product I know works best for me. I do a lot of rework using frisket paper, and the paper tends to leave adhesive residue on anything other than urethane. I also like using a clear that dries rock hard overnight, but not so hard it won't accept recoating. If the clear is too hard (like some of the totally rock hard uro clears), there maybe problems with delamination.

I need a clear on which I can cut frisket, but even more important, something with a very forgiving time window—how long you can wait to spray between coats. Some clears have a very tight window with no wiggle room, while others are more lenient; I need all the help I can get. Custom painting is Murphy's Law to the 100th power. Whatever can go wrong will go wrong—and when it does, it will go *so* wrong that you'll do anything—I mean *anything*—to turn back the clock. So I prefer products that cut me some slack. I never know when I'll need it.

Aaron Stevenson

BEFORE YOU CLEAR

I usually wet sand after I've finished any artwork and have removed the tape or stencil material. I use 800-grit paper and lightly sand only the area that did not receive any artwork, carefully sanding *around* the artwork. This removes any foreign objects or unwanted paint, like overspray or drips that have found their way onto the surface.

Never touch the parts with your bare hands. I keep a clean, wet washcloth in the hand I hold the part with, keeping that against the surface. It prevents anything on my hands from contaminating the part, and also provides a source of water as I wet sand. After wet sanding, I wipe the part down very thoroughly with the wet washcloth, then rinse off the part. Let the parts air dry, but after the parts have dried a bit, use a paper towel and wipe away any remaining water drops and any water that has accumulated on the fender edges. You can use compressed air to blow off the water immediately after wet sanding, but make sure your air source is very clean and well filtered. No sense in blowing dirty, oily air onto a fresh, clean surface. The main reason for removing this water is so minerals in the water won't remain on the parts after the water has dried up. This can be a real problem if your shop is in an area with hard water or if you use well water.

If you're using urethane clear, make sure the catalyst is fresh. I don't use catalyst from a container that has been open for more than two months. If the catalyst has a real syrupy look to it, don't use it. For that matter, always check the appearance of any product you use. If something doesn't look right, trust your instincts—don't use it.

SEALING DOWN ARTWORK
AND FILLER CLEARS

I used to use base coat clear to seal down my artwork. Then I started finding that, in some cases, when I used very thinned-down white airbrushing in my artwork, the base coat clear seemed to wash out the white, muting it. My remedy for that is a risky one. I went straight to coating my artwork with urethane clear. It's risky because the uro clear is heavy, and if not applied carefully, the weight of the clear and flowout can literally drag down the artwork, smearing and running it.

I clear coat the parts using a urethane clear catalyzed with a superfast hardener. Most brands of uro clears have several kinds of hardener that can be used. For example, PPG's 2021 has a superfast hardener called DFX-11 Supercharger. PPG also has a slower hardener, DCX-61, which is best used for finishing clear coats that won't need as many coats as a filler clear. Superfast hardeners dry quicker, but tend to not flow out and give that glasslike finish desired in a final clear. On the other hand, the slower hardener may take a few days to thoroughly dry, but will flow out beautifully and retain that wet look.

Slower hardener also requires more finesse to paint because it has more time to form sags and runs. This can be a real problem on frames and swingarms, as the parts are hit from so many different angles, it's easy to get too much in one area. Be very patient the first time you spray clear on a frame. Have a plan of attack: Decide where the coats will start and the path the spray gun will take as it moves over the parts. This is always easier with color, because you can see the progress as it goes, but clear can be tricky.

If you use urethane clear, two light coats should be sprayed and allowed to set up before heavier coats can be layered on. The first coats must *not* be sprayed too heavy. Use very light but decent-coverage coats that lock down the artwork. I learned this the hard way, having to go back and rework my artwork after heavy coats of uro clear took the uncleared base coat artwork and ran it right down the side of a tank. After spraying the lockdown coats, I lay down a medium coat, then follow that with several heavy coats—heavy enough to flood plenty of clear over the paint edges, but not so heavy that it forms runs or sags.

The next day—or when it is hard enough—I wet sand with 600 grit. If the urethane clear is not hard enough after drying overnight (about eight hours or so), you're using either the wrong clear or the wrong hardener, it was mixed improperly, or the hardener has gone bad. Again, this is where doing test panels to test your product will come in very, very handy. When using a product for the first time, I always test it before using it on a customer's parts. Be careful as you sand. You don't want to sand through any paint edges sticking up, especially if the graphic or flame will not be pinstriped (**see fig. 3**). Again, don't touch the parts or let accumulated water dry on them.

I handle parts from areas that will be covered by their mounting bolts or from underneath, or I use paper towels between my skin and the parts. I never touch a ready-to-clear frame without at least a paper towel between the frame and my hand. The reason is that the few imperfections I have noticed in finished, clear coated paint were caused by fingerprints. It doesn't happen often, but even one time is too many. Take care with every part you paint.

THE JOY OF REWORK

Once you've locked down your artwork, it's time for touching up any ragged lines or places where the flame or graphic is not perfect. For example, if a tail end of a flame is crooked, just widen and lengthen it a bit by taping it off and respraying. Got a ragged line on a graphic? Just tape off the line and touch it up. This is also the time I add shadows under graphics and flames. I just tape off the lines under which I want the shadow, and using very thinned-down black, I airbrush a light shadow along the tape edge.

If you're doing airbrush work, this is a perfect time for rework. Don't like the way that face looks on that eagle you just painted, or unhappy with parts of a mural? Rework it. Tape it off with tape or frisket paper, gently trim away the area you want to work on, and fix it. If you don't like the repair, pull off the tape or frisket and wet sand the rework away with 800 grit, then try again. You won't bother your original artwork underneath. Believe me, you won't be the only one who's ever done rework. It's not too often that my first round of artwork is also my finished product. Consider it a safety net—I always breathe easier knowing I can go back and rework what I've done, sharpening up lines and details.

HOW TO NOT MISS ANY TOUCHUPS

The last time I checked, painters did not have the best short-term memories. Maybe we didn't always use a fresh air respirator, maybe our skin has soaked up too much lacquer thinner, or maybe we had a little too much fun in high school. Whatever the reason, I have an easy trick that helps me remember every raggy little line and blemish, even on a multilayer graphic or flame paint job. Using either a quick rough sketch of the painted part or with digital photos mounted on a clipboard, I'll use markers (in the same colors as each graphic) and label where all the touchups need to be made. If there are only a few spots to fix, or if I'm too lazy to find the colored markers, I'll just note each touchup mark with the color initials: *BK* for black, *WT* for white, etc.

Once you're touched up, it's time for the second round of filler clear. Again, I go easy and light on the first few coats, since I made touchups and don't want them to run.

Aaron Stevenson

4

Aaron Stevenson

And because the paint edge is not as pronounced, the following clear coats don't need to be as numerous or as thick as they were the first round.

But use common sense, as each situation will be different. If you need to do more rework, now is the time. If the clock is ticking and the customer is screaming, and you have to get in that booth and start with the finish clear coats—*and* your last rework doesn't have a big paint edge—airbrush two medium coats of Intercoat or base coat clear over it. This will help lock the rework paint down and smooth the edge, so you can do your finish coats.

Wait until the first coat has dried before you spray the second. Your first coat should be a medium coat; then go into a couple of heavy-flow coats. Just make sure to hit the freshly reworked areas hard enough to smooth over the rework, but not enough to run the paint. Keep in mind that over time, the lines from the rework will start to show through the clear, but this is another personal judgment issue. Each case is different.

FINISH CLEAR COATS

I usually do two different rounds of finishing clear coat (the first using fast hardener, the second using slow hardener,) just to be sure everything stays nice, flat, and glassy. Lacquer paint has one big advantage over urethane. When lacquer is dry, it is real dry. You don't come back in six

months to see lines around every flame edge where the paint has settled, which is not always the case with urethane clear. Deadlines and whiners don't always allow paint to dry properly. It would be nice to spray a few coats of finish uro clear, wait a week, then wet sand it with 600 or 800 grit and spray another round of coats. But this business rarely works like that. More often than not, painters get to spray a clear coat round one day and follow it the next day with the second and final round.

I don't recommend baking custom paint. I find that paint edges, especially those on graphics and flames, are more pronounced on baked paint. I'm sure other painters and I could speculate and argue *why* that happens, but the point is it has happened to me, so I don't bake finish clear coats.

GETTING THAT STUFF TO STICK

Another debate concerns grits used for wet sanding: 600 grit or finer. The surface needs a good enough tooth for the clear to grip, but you don't want to worry about sand scratches appearing in the clear coat surface as it dries. Jon Kosmoski recommends using 600 grit for wet sanding, as anything with finer grit could lead to delamination problems.

But delamination seems to plague places where things bolt against painted surfaces, like mounting bolt areas. On many custom applications, like rear fenders and frames, this can be an especially painful problem. A bolt gets tightened

5

most. And I hate buffing. I know the devil is waiting for me. He's got a buffer with a nasty pad, cheap polish, and an endless mountain of bike parts. I have no choice but to be good. Even with the many handy-dandy tools that make buffing a breeze, I still hate to buff. Maybe there have been too many traumatic buffing experiences in my past.

Too many times I have been finished, and I mean *done*, with a job—then saw one little bit of dust that didn't quite buff all the way flat. I sanded it down just a bit with 2,000 grit, hit it ever so slightly with the buffer, and then watched in horror as a spot opened up, indicating that I had gone through a round of clear coat. Honestly, sometimes I didn't think I would survive having made that mistake. I would stand there, buffer in hand, waiting for my heart to stop. Eventually, my blood would start flowing again. I'd get out the 800-grit sandpaper, wet sand the part, and grimly head back into the booth for another round of clear.

I can't go back there. So I leave buffing duties to someone else, a sturdy young man with a strong heart and a disposition for buffing. So, here's the recipe for buffing from the clear coat master himself, Wayne Springs of Little Rock Auto in Charlotte, North Carolina. "Wet sand bits of dust and other boogers with 2,000 grit. Dry it off, make sure all these bugs are out. I then use Hi Gloss, Clean Cut, Non-Silicone Auto Compound (Number 32101 made by EZ-1, Stockton, California, 209-948-1133). First, I buff out with the Clean Cut to a high gloss using a 3M Perfect-It foam pad No. 05723. Then I switch to a 3M Perfect-It foam pad No. 05725 and go over the parts with 3M Perfect-It Foam Pad Polishing Glaze No. 05996. After that, I wipe the parts down with Meguiar's No. 7 Glaze."

Wayne always amazes me with his clear coats, and a glassy clear coat will bring out all the best qualities of a fantastic paint job.

down against the painted surface, twisting against it, and tears the paint away from the metal. Usually the primer and base coat sticks, and only the urethane paint colors (candy and clear) separate. (This is another point in the base coat painter's favor.) Prime examples are the areas where the seat bolts onto the rear fender, or where the mounting tabs for the front fender bolt to the lower legs. These parts were not designed to have umpteen coats of paint on them. The heavily coated surface gets squished against the mounting, and the many soft coats of urethane puddle up.

I try to somehow apply as little paint on these areas as possible. If I have rear fender artwork I am clearing, especially if I'm trying to smooth out some paint edges, I'll flood the clear only over the artwork, staying away from that seat bolt hole. I also sand the living crap out of any mounting area—the mounting tabs on the gas tank, oil tank, and fenders—each time I sand, starting with the primer coat. But be careful not to sand through on the sharp corners. It takes practice to get good at it. Be patient.

BUFFING

I try to be a good person, because my idea of hell is spending eternity doing the one thing that you absolutely hate the

CHAPTER 16
TROUBLESHOOTING— LIVING TO FIGHT ANOTHER DAY

OK folks, big news, I ain't perfect. I gave up trying to be perfect. But I do try to enjoy what I do, so this chapter deals with trying to fix the problems—imperfections—that happen along the way. These remedies usually work for me. They might be the answer to your problem. Then again, they might not.

In this chapter I will do the best I can to help when the situation seems totally bleak and hopeless. However, there are so many variables in custom painting that it's impossible to cover absolutely every little thing. In the past, books that that have been the most helpful to me were ones with comprehensive troubleshooting pages. Custom painting is 60 percent common sense, 25 percent technique, and 15 percent talent. Being very patient also helps.

COLOR MATCHING AND REPAIRS

Ah, the pure pleasure of matching your custom colors. Sooner or later, all painters find themselves in the position of having to match a custom color they painted. Maybe it's a part that got damaged and the whole part needs to be painted to match. Or maybe the damage is minimal and just a small area on the part needs repainted.

Sometimes painters get inspired while applying coats of paint and throw on a little of this and a little of that and it comes out incredible. So you can't just open up a can of paint and spray away. Hopefully, notes were kept while the color was sprayed and you still have the color sample. Well, notes don't always get taken and they can get lost. And the color sample was not sprayed at the same time as the parts, so there's no guarantee it's a perfect match. Plus, if the job is over a year old, fading might have occurred.

Some painters are great at spot repairing candy colors. Candy can be difficult, and some candy colors are easier to spot repair than others. Unless the repaired area is bordered by artwork, I usually repaint the entire candy-coated area, sometimes masking off the artwork—I usually try to save the artwork if at all possible. Pearl and solid colors are easier to spot repair. But if there are many layers of clear over a lot of artwork, with lighter colors you can sometimes see a shadow where the spot repair meets up with the original paint.

Here's what I do when I have to match an impossible custom color.

I always have a part of the bike to use as a reference. If the customer whines about having to give you two parts off the bike, they're gonna whine a lot more when they get the part back and it's not a perfect match. Do whatever it takes to get the other part. You won't go as insane as you would if you were just trying to match by memory or pictures. Photos usually distort colors. Colors can also fade or change over time.

REPAIRS

If the part is a repaired part, you've probably sanded through several rounds of urethane in feather edging the area. This will appear as "halos" in the surface around the area of the repair. **See fig. 2.** The problem is that

2

Halos.

breaking through the layers can result in the breaks in the layers bleeding up through the primer, right through the color coats. What I do is make sure my last layer of plastic filler is a two-part flowable polyester filler putty. Then I apply a smooth, not overly thick coat of it over any place where I sanded through layers of paint. This tends to seal everything down. I carefully sand the filler with 180-grit paper, so my surface is as even as I can get it without going though any more layers of paint.

Mask off the repair area just beyond—maybe 2 to 3 inches—the plastic fill zone, protecting the paint around the repair. Now do the priming. Sometimes you're trying to save artwork, so there may not be much room. Mask off the artwork. Use your own judgment; each situation is different. Now spray a few coats of a two-part fill primer. Watch the area to see if anything like little cracks appear in the wet surface. This is when you'll see if there's anything going on below all those coats of paint. Sometimes the under coats crack just beyond the dent or damage, but the color and clear coats look fine on the surface. These cracks won't be very noticeable on the sanded surface but with freshly applied paint, you will see them. Stop painting. Any tiny bubbles or lifting areas may mean that a reaction is occurring between the original paint and the repair. If there's anything but a smooth, flawless primed surface, stop painting. Let it dry, and then dig out all the area where the problem appears. Using 80 grit, remove all the problem paint. Feather edge the area. Get out the flowable filler, then fill and cover the newly sanded area. Hopefully this time all the damaged paint will be gone and the repair will hold.

After the priming is done and dry, wet sand with 400 or a similar grit paper that will allow the base coat to stick but not leave deep sand scratches.

COLOR MATCHING

Make sure you are doing your color match on a sunny day. Start first thing in the morning. Afternoon light can have a golden glow that may affect the color match. If the sun hides behind a cloud for the rest of the day, stop painting and check the tech sheet for the paint you are using. It's important to know your product. How long can you let the part sit without sanding if you want to recoat it? With the paint I use, I can let base coat sit 12 hours and urethane three days before recoating without sanding. This is important, because light is critical to matching colors, and you may need time to get the light to cooperate.

Go light on the coats, especially if you're using candy paint. It's better to go too light than too dark or too much—you can always add another coat. Once you've applied too much paint, you're back to square one.

Let the paint dry dust free, but still raw enough to recoat. Bring the part outside the booth and look at it in the sun. Does it match in the sun and in the booth? Hopefully it does, your repair holds, and we all live happily ever after. But don't lose your mind if things go wrong. Say, for example, you have applied just one too many coats of candy. There's not much you can do at that point anyway. Clean the guns, shut down the shop, and try again the next day. Tell your customer you'd rather have it right tomorrow than wrong today.

CAUSE AND EFFECT

There are a great many reasons for things going wrong. When something doesn't look right, stop painting, let it dry for a while, and research the problem. As I said, the answers aren't always easy. But here are a few problems, their *possible* causes, and potential solutions.

CRAZING OR CRACKING

This is usually caused by temperature differences between parts and the paint. If the parts were just removed from a colder section of the shop, and your booth or spray area is warmer, give the parts some time to heat up. Painting cold parts in a warm area with warm paint can result in crazing or cracking. Always let your parts, and your paint, acclimate to your shop temperature before you use them.

The repair for crazing or cracking can be vexing. There aren't many options. Some painters have made saves in this area by recoating the part with over-reduced paint, but I have not had much success with this. I don't like putting hours of artwork over base coats I have doubts with. I usually end up sanding down the cracks, sealing, and starting over. In my early painting days, I made a few trips to the sandblaster with crazed parts. If the crazing covers the entire part, sandblasting may be the best option.

WRINKLING

Wrinkling is usually caused by trapped solvents or repenetration. When this occurs, you've used the wrong temperature range of reducer, you've recoated too soon, or it's simply way too hot to be painting.

Some painters mistakenly use a cold (fast) reducer to dry their work quicker. This is a very bad idea, because the top dries faster and the bottom of the layer (or coat) just lies there. The drier, top layer acts as a lid, so the bottom layer can't evaporate the solvents, and they just lie there, soaking into the layer below. If you recoat before this layer has completely dried, at the least you'll end up with wrinkles, and at the worst, lifts—clear to the primer, and maybe even to the metal! Ouch.

Painting Rules Number 3 and Number 1 apply in this situation. This is what happens when trying to take short-cuts. Having mishmash layers of catalyzed and uncatalyzed paint, clear, primer, and sealer is unstable. There's no telling what may happen down the road, even if it looks good. If you have any doubts, remove all the paint, right down to the substrate.

Some company's products can be more prone to wrinkling. This is due to the temperature of their solvents. Some paints are pretty "hot" and thoroughly penetrate the layers below; with products like this, time between coats is crucial. The window between coats is very strict. If you wait a few minutes too long, it wrinkles, and if you lay too heavy a coat, it wrinkles. This is especially a problem with urethane paints.

I make every effort to use paints that are very forgiving so I don't have to deal with this sort of problem. This is why testing your paint products is so important. A few hours testing can really save you time, money, and sanity. When I use a new product, I put it through a few tests, deliberately abusing the product, trying to *make* it wrinkle on a sample part. This is a way of exploring your boundaries without using expensive motorcycle parts, and your time, as guinea pigs.

Other causes for wrinkling are bad catalyst and uncured or soft urethane. Wrinkling can also happen when you're painting base coat over a urethane clear that is over another base coat. It begins when solvent from the top layer of base coat gets through the urethane clear in a thin or broken spot and resaturates the base coat underneath the clear. Now there's a layer of catalyzed clear between two wet layers of base coat.

I have never been able to save paint that has wrinkled. Again, I hate trying some last-ditch effort, having it look all right, then in a few days—Whammo!—it's showing the wrinkled effect again, but now it's under all kinds of clear and the customer is due to arrive shortly. If I have any doubts as to whether my efforts will be 100 percent successful, it's back to Rule Number 1; I'll take it down to the metal and remove those doubts.

OK, so what should you do if it wrinkles? If the entire part is wrinkled, sandblast and start over. Don't waste any more time. In cases where there's just a bit of wrinkling on one part, let it dry and remove the damaged paint by wet sanding. Let the part dry out thoroughly, in case any of the under coats are soft, and examine them very closely. Are there still tiny wrinkles in them? If not, use flowable polyester filler to cover up all the layers you sanded through, because those separations between the layers might show through the base coats I'm about to reapply. Sand the filler, lay on some two-part primer, let dry, sand again, then apply epoxy primer sealer immediately before spraying the new base coat. Make sure you give the sealer enough time to dry; the stuff I use says to wait at least 15 minutes but no more than 12 hours. I wait 30 minutes. Then look very closely around the edges of the repair for tiny wrinkles after resuming your paint application.

RUNS AND SAGS

If you've got runs or sags, you applied the paint too heavily or you over-reduced for the conditions. **See fig. 3.** Maybe you used the wrong temperature of reducer and the paint is drying too slowly.

To make these disappear, carefully sand the high spots. I'll wrap 600-grit sandpaper over Motor Guard Company's aluminum sanding blocks (Run Blockers) and slowly wet sand down the sag, taking care not to sand anything other than the run itself. It's too easy to get light spots around a run that was sanded away, especially in candy. I take the run down with the hard block, and then softly sand the whole area with a finer-grit paper, sometimes using a Motor Guard flexible pad.

Beware if candy paint was run along a fender edge. Chances are you might sand through the candy and create a light spot. When that happens, I leave the run alone and do my filler clear coats to build up the area around the run. Then I sand it later, when there's less chance of getting into the candy coats. For big drips off the edges of parts, I use a new razor blade to shave off the run, then carefully wet sand the edge smooth.

BUBBLES IN CLEAR

When you get big bubbles, what you have is lifting paint, which is a serious delamination problem. **See fig. 4.** There

are several possible causes. Sometimes these bubbles are caused by the paint lifting and not adhering to the layer below it. Many others are caused by some kind of solvent problems. The remedy? You need to entirely remove the affected area. Let the paint dry and sand it off. In extreme cases concerning candy urethane or clear, it might be best to use a razor blade and literally peel the parts. I've been there; I've done that; I've felt like screaming and running into the night. Once you get the paint off the part, you need to spend some time to figure out why the paint did not stick in the first place.

Small bumpy bubbles are an entirely different animal. Sometimes you'll see a small bump in the paint that almost looks like a speck of dust. If you poke at it and it flexes inward, it is a bubble. Somehow, the paint did not stick in that spot.

If there are a whole bunch of them, get out the 400 grit and take down the surface, removing all the color coats. Look carefully at the primer layer. Did the problem start there? Are there any suspicious areas or marks in the primer?

If you have only one or two bubbles, you may be able to save it. Using a stencil knife, dig out the bubble. Try to see what caused it. Then wrap some 220-grit paper around a pen and carefully sand out the little pit you dug, smoothing the edges the best you can. Sand the area around the pit with 400 grit. Using polyester filler, fill the tiny hole, making sure the filler runs over the edge. Let it dry thoroughly. Sand and feather it *without* going through to the edge or disturbing the surrounding surface—you don't want deep scratches in the paint you are trying to save. Tape and paper off the area, and spot prime it with two-part primer. Wet sand it, then spot in the base color. After you make the repair, wet sand everything *but* the repair with 600 grit. Reason? There's a

good chance overspray has found its way onto the surface past the repair. Since the base coat was cleared after the color coats were done, there is room to sand.

If you have any candy layers, I recommend redoing the entire base coat process from scratch unless you're a whiz at repairing candy. Some painters are great at spot repairing candy colors, and some candy colors are easier to spot repair than others. Solid and pearl colors are a little easier. You should be able to spot paint the repair. If the lifting bubbles appear all over the part? Remove all the paint by sandblasting and start over.

Sometimes lifted paint bubbles appear only over areas where bodywork was done. Usually the problem is with the hardener used with plastic filler. Maybe it was old, or maybe it was just plain bad. If this is the place you're at, refer to Rule Number 1 again: Sandblast! *Don't* try to spot repair, or problems related to sanding through all the paint layers will haunt you. Just give in, blast all that paint and body work off, buy new filling material, and try again. Do not use the material you used before and do not just buy new hardener, especially if the filler used was over a year old.

Itty, bitty bubbles locked in the clear coat itself are usually cause by solvent-drying problems. I normally run into this problem with candy and clear coats in the summer when it's hot and the humidity is high. So what's the remedy? Stop painting. Let it dry and then wet sand the affected areas. Sand away the coats containing the bubbles, then repaint. This time make sure you're using the proper temperature of

reducer for the conditions, and that you don't wait too long in between coats. Don't apply the coats too heavily, and don't do too many coats in one day. On hot, humid days, I make every effort to be done with my candy or clear coat process in an hour or less.

STRANGE MARKS UNDER CLEAR COATS

Weeks or months after the job is completed, mystical fingerprints will sometimes appear in the paint or under the clear. Hey, nobody's perfect. And what's worse, there's no easy answer here, just hard work. Some colors can be spot repaired. But take note, sometimes the rework can cause a shadow with certain light colors that have tons of clear coat on them. This is due to the rework being up on the thick clear coats, separated from the base coat by the thick clear.

If a spot repair is not possible, on a *sunny* day, I wet sand the part in the sun with 600-grit paper, carefully rinsing and watching as I go. What I'm doing is sanding down through my clear coats to the surface or layer that the fingerprint is on. Hopefully it's sitting on top of a clear coat, and not under or within the color coats. The clear coat is where it usually happens. If it is indeed trapped in the clear coat, I sand it off, then feather the surrounding layers of clear. I spot spray the area with filler clear (I use uro clear) until it is level, and then reclear the whole part. If the mark is under candy coat, you're S.O.L. Do not pass go, and do not collect $200. Start over by either spot repairing or redoing the base coat. Whichever is applicable.

PULLING UP TAPE—AND PAINT ALONG WITH IT

Start by saying a quick prayer that this is only happening in this one spot. Look at the edges of the spot. Use a stencil knife to poke the broken edge and see if the whole layer is lifting. Hopefully you did everything correctly, thoroughly sanding all the coats that needed to be sanded with the proper grit paper. If so, then this may just be an isolated incident. Feather edge the area. If the repair area is deep, fill the pit with polyester filler, tape it off, spot prime, spot paint, and rework the artwork.

If you took shortcuts, if you're not 100 percent sure of the adhesion of the paint layers, or if someone else did the base coats, there's a serious problem. Stick 2-inch tape onto the part, let it sit a while, then rip off the tape. In short, test the part to see if the problem keeps happening. If it does, remove all the paint. I know this sounds drastic, especially if hours of artwork are on the surface, but keep in mind, even if you spot repair the affected areas, there's a very good chance there will be problems down the road. Fix it now or fix it later.

DRIPPED OR SPILLED PAINT ON A FRESHLY AIRBRUSHED SURFACE

Let dripped paint dry. **See fig. 5.** Hopefully there are lots of clear coat layers protecting the base coat color. Damp sand off any paint on the unairbrushed surface and rework

any artwork. Don't worry if you can still see an outline of the drip. After you clear coat, just retouch that area again with the airbrush and it will be perfect.

If the drip or spill is on the clear, just let it dry and wet sand it off. Sometimes it can be quickly wiped off.

WHAT YOU SHOULD NEVER DO

As a rule, I do not bake parts that have artwork. Not even in a professional bake booth. And never, never, never bake paint in the sun. I tried it once. It was an extremely bad idea. Evil bubbles appeared, and I had to invoke my Painting Rule Number 1 *yet again*. I don't know why it happened, although I'm sure someone could explain it to me. That was eight years ago. Ever since, I dry my paint in my shed or in the shade—that is, after the paint has sat in the booth and dried enough to remove the parts from the paint stands. I never let paint that's less than two weeks old sit in the sun for any length of time.

AIRBRUSH PROBLEMS

Let's start with the easy ones. Use common sense when troubleshooting airbrush problems. Stay calm and investigate the problem, thinking it through. And always protect the business end of the airbrush. Keep protective caps in place when brushes are not being used at that moment.

Solutions to airbrush problems depend on some degree on the type of airbrush you're using, but keeping the airbrush very clean is the best way to keep it working properly. At the beginning of each airbrush session, I always remove the needle and give it a quick wipe with thinner just to head off any potential problems before I start. What follows are a few typical airbrush problems, their causes, and their remedies.

Problem One: If paint is spitting out of the airbrush and the paint is very grainy, and doesn't have an even, smooth flow, the paint is too thick. Either the air pressure is too low, or you need to thin down the paint.

Problem Two: If paint comes out of the airbrush even when you're not pulling the trigger, it could be one of two problems. Cause 1: Something, maybe dried paint, a hair, a fiber, whatever, is caught in the tip, causing the needle to not close into the tip properly. Remedy 1: Remove the needle and the tip and clean both very thoroughly. Very carefully, use an old airbrush needle to poke into the tip and see if there's anything caught in the passage. Cause 2: Wear and tear on needle and/or the tip is causing paint to escape through those gaps created by the wear. (This could also be caused by paint leaking into air passages—see Problem Six below.) Remedy 2: Replace the worn parts. Replace the needle first, and if the problem is still present, replace the tip.

6

An important note on tip repair: Some tips are threaded into place and you need to use the little wrench that came with the airbrush to unscrew the tip. Other tips are simply press fit—pushed in place and held there by friction. Take great care with those, because they can fall out very easily when working on the airbrush. Work over a towel, so the tip won't roll away and be lost forever.

Problem Three: If no paint comes out of the airbrush, or if the trigger must be pulled back farther than normal to get paint flow, something is probably caught in one of the paint passages. You will need to remove the needle and tip and clean them thoroughly. Also clean out the paint passages in the airbrush body. If using a bottle feed airbrush, see Problem Five.

Problem Four: When the airflow is not consistent, it's usually because the spray regulator or airbrush head is not sealing properly, causing outside air to affect airflow. Either one could be loose, or with some airbrushes, the head washer could be worn. To fix this, remove the spray regulator or the head. Make sure the sealing surfaces are clean and free of debris. Replace the head washer, if applicable.

Problem Five: No paint comes out when you're using a bottle-feed airbrush. This happens all the time. Either the tube or siphon cap is clogged, or the air hole in top of the cap is clogged. Check and clean the paint passage up from the bottle and clear out the air hole for good flow through the bottle.

Problem Six: The needle does not move smoothly when pulled back. Remove the needle and clean it. That may be all it needs. But check the trigger area in the airbrush body. There could be paint that is leaking back past the needle seal and is now sticking in the machinery that pulls the needle back. Great. Just great. When this happens to me, I usually buy a new airbrush, and then renew my efforts to try not to let very reduced paint sit in the airbrush for a long period of time. Very reduced paint will leak out faster than thick paint and cause you problems.

In some airbrushes the seal is not too hard to replace. In others it is a total pain. If paint has been leaking into these areas, the seal or packing that seals the head from the body is worn. Paint leaking into the airbrush body can also leak into the air passages. Clean out the body, and if possible, take apart the air inlet and clean it. You'll need to remove the needle, needle chuck, and spring assembly. Take the whole assembly apart and clean it thoroughly. Remove the trigger mechanism and clean out the inner airbrush body with cotton swabs. Use a small, round brush to clean out the needle chucking guide. Once everything looks factory new, reassemble it all. Reinstall the trigger and blow air through the brush until it comes out clean. But chances are it will keep happening, unless the seal is changed.

INDEX

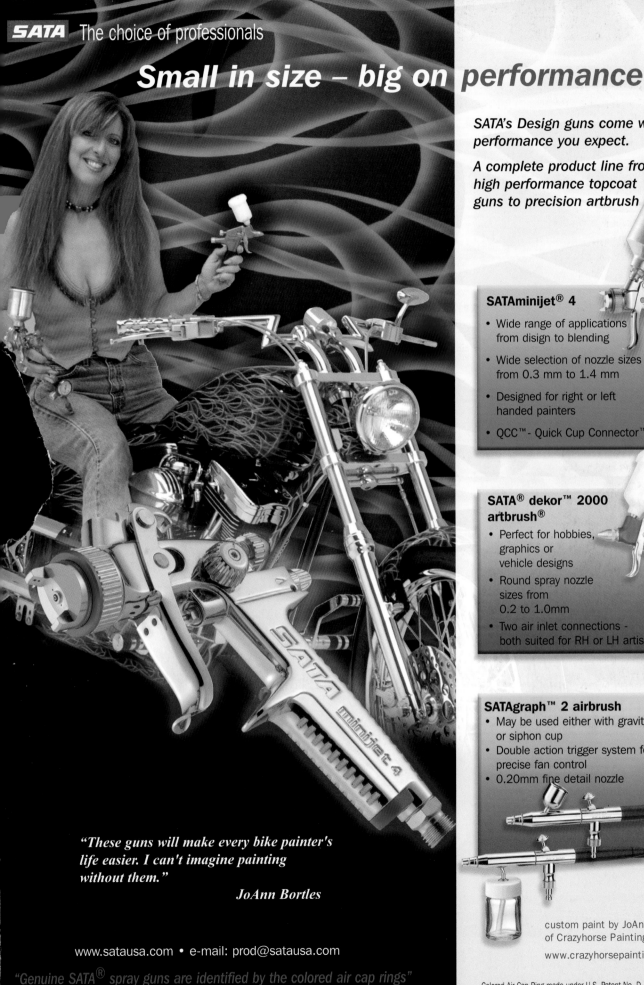
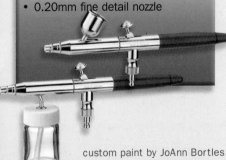

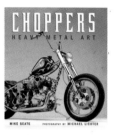
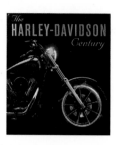

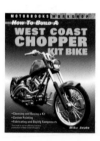
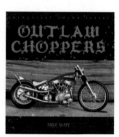

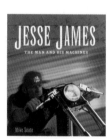